TOTAL BASEBALL TRIVIA

The Editors of Total Baseball

KINGSTON, NEW YORK   TOTAL Sports Illustrated   NEW YORK, NEW YORK

For information about permission to reproduce selections from this book,
please write to:

Permissions
Total Sports Publishing
100 Enterprise Drive
Kingston, New York 12401

www.TotalBaseballTrivia.com
www.TotalSportsPublishing.com

Cover design: Todd Radom
Interior design: C. Linda Dingler

Printed in Canada

ISBN: 1-930844-02-6

Library of Congress Cataloging-in-Publication Data

Total baseball trivia / by the editors of Total baseball
    p. cm.
  ISBN 1-930844-02-6 (pbk.)
   1. Baseball--United States--Miscellanea. I. Total baseball.

 GV873 .T69 2001
 796.357--dc21

                                                    00-054431

PREFACE

Total Baseball Trivia was born at one of our editorial staff's weekly meetings. As we waited for everyone to filter in, we probably talked about trade rumors, the previous night's games, maybe Chuck Knoblauch's latest fielding adventure. But, as always, we managed to squeeze in some baseball trivia.

These pre-meeting trivia sessions jumped from Pedro Martinez to Turkey Stearnes to the Cleveland Spiders to Rob Deer without causing a ripple in the flow of conversation. At this particular meeting, during the usual quizzing, someone suggested that "we could make a book out of this stuff." *Total Baseball Trivia* is that book.

We compiled 360 questions from every era of the game's history, shooting for a good mix of old and recent, statistical and biographical. The questions vary in degree of difficulty, which you'll see reflected in their point values. Multiple choice questions have lower values, since they all present a 25 percent chance of a correct answer.

Some of the questions may predate their reader, and some are just downright difficult—but the harder the question, the higher the reward. So whether you're alternating home-and-visitor with a friend, or just scoring the whole nine innings for yourself—give every question your best shot. Many of them offer partial credit; in other words, naming every player who won back-to-back MVP Awards may seem daunting, but if you can name some of them you'll still get points.

We suggest using some device, maybe an index card, to

slide down the answer pages. That way you won't see the answers to questions you haven't read yet. All answers can be found at the back of the book, and you can use your card to mark your place in the answer section. Inning-by-inning scoresheets can also be found at the back of the book.

Keep in mind that *Total Baseball Trivia* wasn't designed for someone to "ace." Any "baseball expert" would be hard-pressed to answer a lot of these questions correctly. So don't get too frustrated if you're swinging and missing at more of these than you expected. Your reading of the answer may well show you something about the game that you didn't know before—whether you got the points or not.

Best of luck.

THE EDITORS OF TOTAL BASEBALL
December 2000

TOTAL BASEBALL TRIVIA

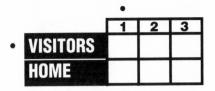

	1	2	3
VISITORS			
HOME			

1ST INNING

Top 1st

1. At each position on the diamond there is at least one player who won back-to-back MVPs. At first base and center field there are two players who won back-to back MVPs. Name them. (5 of 11: *3 points*; 7 of 11: *4 points*; 9 of 11: *7 points*; 11 of 11: *9 points*)

2. Who were the only two men to play for the Yankees, Dodgers, Giants, and Mets? (*4 points*)

3. On December 13, 1956, the Brooklyn Dodgers traded Jackie Robinson to the New York Giants, but the deal fell through when Robinson announced his retirement. Who was he going to be traded for? (*6 points*)

4. Four players in history have had 30-plus homers and hitting streaks of 30 or more in the same season. Two of them are active—name them. (*4 points*)

5. Which Hall of Fame pitcher did Christy Mathewson defeat for his final major league victory? (*4 points*)

    A) Mordecai Brown
    B) Grove Cleveland Alexander
    C) Eppa Rixey
    D) Walter Johnson

6. In 1997 Mark McGwire hit 24 homers with St. Louis after starting the season with 34 as a member of the Oakland A's. Which of the following players matched that feat of hitting 20 or more home runs for two different teams during the same season? (*3 points*)

    A) Dave Kingman
    B) Fred McGriff
    C) Mike Piazza
    D) David Justice

7. Who was the first relief pitcher to win the Cy Young Award? (*4 points*)

8. Who was the first player to lead both leagues in home runs in his career? (*5 points*)

9. Name the last player to hit home runs in his first two major league at bats. (*4 points*)

10. On June 8, 1961, the Milwaukee Braves became the first team to hit four consecutive home runs in one inning. Who hit them? (3 of 4: 5 points; 4 of 4: 7 points)

11. What player had the most walks in a season without hitting a home run? (8 points)

12. In 1997 the Los Angeles Dodgers' starting rotation featured five pitchers from five different countries. Name the countries. (4 of 5: 4 points; 5 of 5: 5 points)

13. What was the only decade that didn't have a seven-game World Series? (4 points)

14. Who was Cal Ripken's double play partner the night he broke Lou Gehrig's consecutive games record in 1995? (3 points)

    A) Billy Ripken
    B) Floyd Rayford
    C) Roberto Alomar
    D) Manny Alexander

15. Among players whose last name begins with "E," which two players are first and second all-time in homers? (*6 points*)

16. Who holds the record for most consecutive years leading his league in stolen bases? (*4 points*)

17. I led the National League in strikeouts seven years in a row, won 50 games in a two-year span, captured three ERA titles, and won an MVP. I was both a founding member of the "Daffiness Boys" and a latecomer to the "Gashouse Gang." I did not pitch in the World Series until I was 43 years old. Who am I? (*3 points*)

18. In 2000 the Braves became the second team in history to have three relievers with 12 or more saves. What was the first team? (*7 points*)

19. Which of these teams finished last in the first 10-team league of the 20th century? (*4 points*)

    A) New York Mets
    B) Kansas City Athletics
    C) Kansas City Royals
    D) Montreal Expos

20. What stadium played host to the first major league game on the West Coast? (*6 points*)

Bottom 1st

1. Who had more at bats before age 25 than any other player in history? (*5 points*)

2. Who was Major League Baseball's commissioner between the reigns of Ford Frick and Bowie Kuhn? (*4 points*)

3. In which situation did National League starting pitchers have the lowest overall ERA in 1999? (*2 points*)

    A) Three or fewer days rest
    B) Four days rest
    C) Five days rest
    D) Six or more days rest

4. I was the winner in the final game of the 1949 season that sent my team to the World Series and sent Boston home. From 1949–53 I had a 92–40 record and was on a world champion each year. They called me the "Springfield Rifle," but specialized in beating New York teams in the World Series. Who am I? (*5 points*)

5. Jeff Bagwell played 136 games for New Britain in his last minor league season in 1990. How many home runs did he hit? (*6 points*)

6. Which major league rival of both the National and American Leagues featured future Hall of Famers such as Mordecai "Three Finger" Brown, Joe Tinker, and Eddie Plank? (*3 points*)

    A) National Association
    B) American Association
    C) Federal League
    D) Continental League

7. The last four pitchers to go 14 innings in a start all played for the same team in the same year. Name the team. (*6 points*)

8. In 1956 there was one player in each league that hit 40 or more home runs. Name the two players. (*4 points*)

9. I pitched the Washington Senators to their last pennant. I won a combined 50 games between 1932 and 1933, leading the American League in wins both seasons and also pitching in a league-best 52 games in '33. They called me "the General" after the man who originated the draft lottery in World War I. Who am I? (*5 points*)

    A) Walter Johnson
    B) Earl Whitehill
    C) Alvin Crowder
    D) Joe Coleman

10. These two teammates were both among the American League leaders in home runs in 2000—one of them earned approximately $5,800 per homer, while the other earned about $310,000 per homer. Who are they? (*4 points*)

11. What St. Louis Cardinal led the National League in on-base percentage in 1987? (*6 points*)

12. Two players in major league history have hit pinch-hit home runs in both games of a doubleheader. Name them. (*7 points*)

13. Match these hitters of World Series game-winning home runs with the pitchers who gave them up.
(5 of 7: *5 points*; 6 of 7: *6 points*; 7 of 7: *8 points*)

1) Carlton Fisk	a) Dennis Eckersley
2) Tommy Henrich	b) Pat Darcy
3) Joe Carter	c) Don Newcombe
4) Kirk Gibson	d) Bob Grim
5) Bill Mazeroski	e) Mitch Williams
6) Eddie Matthews	f) Bob Lemon
7) Dusty Rhodes	g) Ralph Terry

14. Name the only person to be enshrined in the Baseball, Pro Football, and National College Football halls of fame. (*5 points*)

15. Ivan Rodriguez threw out the highest percentage of runners in the AL in 1999, with 52.8 percent. Who ranked second in the league in that statistic? (*6 points*)

16. Who was the first pitcher to throw a no-hitter and not come to bat in the game? (*4 points*)

A) Rick Wise
B) Vida Blue
C) Nolan Ryan
D) Steve Busby

17. Who pinch ran for Ray Chapman after he was fatally beaned by Carl Mays on August 16, 1920? (*5 points*)

A) Tris Speaker
B) Joe Sewell
C) Harry Lunte
D) Smokey Joe Wood

18. What team was the first to win a World Series game indoors? (*5 points*)

19. Name the only big league ballplayer to ever win a major billiards championship. (*7 points*)

20. Who saved 36 games in his first full season to set a major league record for most saves by a rookie? (*3 points*)

    A) Todd Worrell
    B) Gregg Olson
    C) Rollie Fingers
    D) John Franco

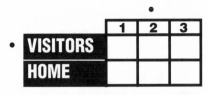

2ND INNING

Top 2nd

1. Among players whose last names begin with "S," who are first, second, and third in all-time home runs? (2 of 3: *5 points*; 3 of 3: *7 points*)

2. Who is the only player to be a member of baseball halls of fame in three countries? (*5 points*)

3. Which of the following Cincinnati players did *not* earn $5,000,000 in salary in 1999? (*3 points*)

    A) Barry Larkin
    B) Juan Guzman
    C) Denny Neagle
    D) Mark Wohlers

4. Name the four teams Roger Maris played for. (*3 points*)

5. Ty Cobb won 12 American League batting titles in 13 seasons between 1907–19. Who interrupted his string in 1916? (*6 points*)

6. Texas's Scott Sheldon and Detroit's Shane Halter recently became the third and fourth players to play all nine positions in a game. Who were the first two players to accomplish the feat? (*5 points*)

7. Which of these catchers named Johnny did *not* win a Gold Glove Award in the 1960s? (*4 points*)

    A) Johnny Blanchard
    B) Johnny Bench
    C) Johnny Edwards
    D) Johnny Roseboro

8. Who is the only pitcher in the Hall of Fame with a losing record? (*6 points*)

9. There are 10 players with four or less letters in their last names who hit 40 homers in a season. Name them. (7 of 10: *6 points*; 8 of 10: *8 points*; 10 of 10: *10 points*)

10. I allowed Jimmy Piersall's 100th career home run and watched in disgust as he ran around the bases backwards. I later became a manager, and in my first full year as skipper brought my team the first world championship in their 98-year history; it also turned out to be the only time I ever managed a 162-game schedule. Who am I? (*5 points*)

11. Who pitched in the 1981 Little League World Series but did not make his professional pitching debut until the 2000 season? (*3 points*)

    A) Chuck Smith
    B) Jim Morris
    C) Derek Bell
    D) Brent Mayne

12. What brothers were the first to pitch against each other in an All-Star Game? (*4 points*)

13. Who stole the most bases in the 1990s? (*4 points*)

14. On August 17, 1973, Don Gullett of the Reds surrendered the 660th and final home run hit by Willie Mays. Which Hall of Fame pitcher surrendered the first? (*6 points*)

15. Who was the last pitcher to throw 300 innings in a season? (*4 points*)

    A) Randy Jones, 1976
    B) Steve Rogers, 1977
    C) Phil Niekro, 1979
    D) Steve Carlton, 1980

16. Anaheim's Darin Erstad had 240 hits in 2000. Who was the only other player to get 240 or more hits while playing a 162-game schedule? (*5 points*)

17. Seventeen players have recorded two hits in an inning of a World Series game. One of them was a pitcher. Who was it? (*5 points*)

    A) Dizzy Dean
    B) Ron Darling
    C) Bob Gibson
    D) Greg Maddux

18. Only three shortstops in major league history have won six or more consecutive Gold Glove Awards. Name them. (*6 points*)

19. In 1963 Sandy Koufax won the pitching Triple Crown by leading the National League in wins, strikeouts, and ERA. He would repeat the feat in 1965 and '66. Koufax was the first National Leaguer to win the Triple Crown in more than 20 years; who was the last NL pitcher to win it before Koufax? (*6 points*)

20. Most fans know that Ted Williams was the last player in the 20th century to hit .400, but who was the first player in the 20th century to reach that mark?   (*3 points*)

   A) Honus Wagner
   B) Ed Delahanty
   C) Napoleon Lajoie
   D) Ty Cobb

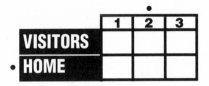

	1	2	3
VISITORS			
HOME			

Bottom 2nd

1. Which team defeated the Arizona Diamondbacks in their inaugural game on March 31, 1998? (*4 points*)

    A) Colorado Rockies
    B) New York Mets
    C) Los Angeles Dodgers
    D) Tampa Bay Devil Rays

2. Who was the oldest player to make his major league debut? (*5 points*)

3. Fill in the missing name in this sequence: Sammy Vick, _____, George Selkirk. (*6 points*)

4. Name the only pitcher to get a win in both the 1985 and 1987 World Series. (*5 points*)

5. I only played 10 years in the major leagues, yet I am a member of the Hall of Fame. I tied or led the National League in home runs for seven consecutive years, and led the league in slugging average and walks three times each. I later joined an expansion team as an announcer and remained with the club for close to 40 years. Who am I? (*3 points*)

6. Who is the only player to hit a home run in his only career World Series at bat? (*5 points*)

    A) Ken O'Dea
    B) Bill Bathe
    C) Jim Mason
    D) Pat Collins

7. Who was the last player to steal 100 bases in a season? (*3 points*)

8. At the infamous 10-cent beer night in Cleveland, the fans rioted in the ninth inning and forced the Indians to forfeit the game on June 4, 1974. Which club received the benefit of this forfeit? (*6 points*)

9. Among players whose last names begin with "O," who are first and second in all-time home runs? (*5 points*)

10. Who was the last player to hit 20 triples in a season? (*4 points*)

11. Who was the last player to hit over .400 and not win his league's batting title? (*4 points*)

    A) Joe Jackson
    B) Ty Cobb
    C) Ted Williams
    D) Rogers Hornsby

12. Name the only player to play for a team in each of the four divisions in one season (in the four-division era, 1969–93). (*5 points*)

13. Although Cy Young won—and lost—more games (511–316) than any other pitcher in major league history, he was 10th on the all-time list of appearances through the end of the 2000 season. Which of the following pitchers did *not* exceed Young's total of 906 appearances? (*5 points*)

    A) Jesse Orosco
    B) Hoyt Wilhelm
    C) Tommy John
    D) Dennis Eckersley

14. There have been seven players who hit 40 homers in a season without knocking in 100 runs. Who are they? (5 of 7: *5 points*; 6 of 7: *6 points*; 7 of 7: *9 points*)

15. Who won 20 games in a season with the highest ERA? (*7 points*)

16. Who was the last player-manager to lead his team to a world championship? (*5 points*)

17. In 1920 George Sisler set a major league mark with 257 hits in a season. Whose record did he break? (*5 points*)

    A) Jesse Burkett
    B) Willie Keeler
    C) Napoleon Lajoie
    D) Ty Cobb

18. What 20th century team had the biggest drop in winning percentage from one year to the next? (*5 points*)

19. What 20th century team had the biggest increase in winning percentage from one year to the next? (*5 points*)

20. In 1951, after many years of dominance, the US All-Stars lost to a Japanese team for the first time. Who was the losing pitcher in Japan's landmark win? (*4 points*)

    A) Lefty Gomez
    B) Bobby Shantz
    C) Lefty O'Doul
    D) Don Newcombe

3RD INNING

Top 3rd

1. Who led all third basemen in RBIs in 2000? (*4 points*)

2. Who was the first player to earn a $1 million annual salary? (*4 points*)

    A) Mike Schmidt
    B) Nolan Ryan
    C) Reggie Jackson
    D) Catfish Hunter

3. Who hit more home runs in his 40s than any other player? (*5 points*)

4. What player had the most doubles in a season without hitting a home run? (*7 points*)

5. Who was the first player to hit home runs in his first two World Series at bats? (*4 points*)

    A) Sal Bando
    B) Joe Rudi
    C) Gene Tenace
    D) Andruw Jones

6. Following the 1984 Olympic Games, the 1985 free-agent draft was loaded with major league talent. The first three position players chosen were B.J. Surhoff, Will Clark, and Barry Larkin, with the first, second, and fourth picks. Who was the first pitcher selected, at pick No. 3? (*6 points*)

7. Name the team for which all nine players made their major league debuts on May 18, 1912. (*6 points*)

8. Which pitcher appeared in the most games over any five-year span? (*4 points*)

    A) Kent Tekulve
    B) Jesse Orosco
    C) Dennis Cook
    D) Rollie Fingers

9. Among players whose last name begins with the letter "A," who is second in home runs? (*7 points*)

10. Who was the National League Rookie of the Year in 1988? (*5 points*)

11. I hit four pinch-hit home runs in 1959 and again in 1960, but I was also a starting first baseman during my career. I was the only starting player on the Reds not to be voted to start the 1957 All-Star Game (two teammates were subsequently stripped of All-Star status by Commissioner Ford Frick due to "ballot stuffing"). Who am I? (*4 points*)

    A) Gus Bell
    B) George Crowe
    C) Wally Post
    D) Wes Covington

12. In 1982 the Chicago Cubs acquired Ryne Sandberg from Philadelphia as a throw-in prospect in a shortstop-for-shortstop trade. Name the two shortstops. (*4 points*)

13. Who was the last lone inductee to the Baseball Hall of Fame? (*5 points*)

14. Name the four players with 10 or more letters in their last names who hit 40 homers in a season.
(3 of 4: *5 points*; 4 of 4: *6 points*)

15. Who played in each of the New York Mets' first 18 years of existence? (*3 points*)

    A) Tom Seaver
    B) Ed Kranepool
    C) Al Jackson
    D) Jerry Grote

16. What second-place team finished the most games behind the division winner? (*7 points*)

17. Who was the last starter to go 15 innings in a game? (*4 points*)

    A) Phil Niekro
    B) Curt Schilling
    C) Bob Lemon
    D) Gaylord Perry

18. What team did four of the five all-time leaders in saves all play for? (*4 points*)

19. Several teams have had starting outfields whose members were subsequently enshrined in the Hall of Fame. Most of those outfields, however, lasted for only a single season. Name the only team whose Hall of Fame outfield remained intact for five full seasons. (*8 points*)

20. What player wore his birthday on the back of his uniform? (*3 points*)

	1	2	3
VISITORS			
HOME			

Bottom 3rd

1. Who surrendered Reggie Jackson's third home run in Game 6 of the 1977 World Series? (*4 points*)

    A) Burt Hooton
    B) Charlie Hough
    C) Don Sutton
    D) Bob Welch

2. Ozzie Smith and Terry Pendleton occupied the left side of the infield for the St. Louis Cardinals for seven years, from 1984–90, winning nine gold gloves between them over that span. Which new infielder broke up that tandem in 1991? (*5 points*)

3. Between 1949–63 only one manager not leading the Yankees won an American League pennant. Who was it? (*4 points*)

    A) Leo Durocher
    B) Lou Boudreau
    C) Al Lopez
    D) Paul Richards

4. Joe DiMaggio's 56-game hitting streak in 1941 is the longest in major league history. Two other American League players have had streaks of 40 or more games. Name them. (*6 points*)

5. Who had the highest single-season winning percentage of any 20-game winner in the 20th century? (*5 points*)

6. Which expansion team had the most wins in its first year of existence? (*3 points*)

    A) Los Angeles Angels
    B) Seattle Mariners
    C) Florida Marlins
    D) Arizona Diamondbacks

7. Who managed the most games without ever finishing in first place? (*6 points*)

8. In 2000 I led all major league outfielders in on-base percentage and slugging average. Who am I? (*5 points*)

9. Hall of Famer Rube Waddell and his catcher, Ossee Schreckengost, were roommates when the Philadelphia Athletics went on the road. In 1904 Schreckengost refused to re-sign with the A's unless a certain clause was inserted into both his and Waddell's contracts. What was the clause? (*8 points*)

10. Who finished in the top five in MVP voting more than any other player? (*5 points*)

    A) Stan Musial
    B) Ted Williams
    C) Mickey Mantle
    D) Willie Mays

11. Among players whose last names begin with "T," who are first and second in all-time home runs? (*6 points*)

12. Before the Braves defeated the Pirates in the National League Championship Series in 1991, when was the last time the franchise had won a postseason game? (*4 points*)

   A) 1957
   B) 1958
   C) 1969
   D) 1982

13. When the 1906 Cubs, winners of 118 games, fell prey to the "Hitless Wonder" White Sox in the World Series, which Cub wore an 0-for-21 collar in the six-game Series? (*5 points*)

   A) Joe Tinker
   B) Hack Wilson
   C) Heinie Zimmerman
   D) Jimmy Sheckard

14. What Hall of Fame pitcher surrendered 500 home runs in his career? (*4 points*)

15. Only one player has scored 150 runs in a season since 1950. Name him. (*4 points*)

16. Who was the first pitcher to win the MVP Award? (*5 points*)

17. Nomar Garciaparra became the first righthanded hitter to win back-to-back American League batting titles since Joe DiMaggio did it in 1939–40. Three righthanded hitters have won back-to-back NL batting crowns since 1940. Name them. (2 of 3: *5 points*; 3 of 3: *6 points*)

18. Most baseball fans know that Pete Rose broke Ty Cobb's career hit record, but whose record did Cobb break? (*5 points*)

    A) Cap Anson
    B) Napoleon Lajoie
    C) Honus Wagner
    D) Tris Speaker

19. What percentage of 20th century World Series were won by a team that led its league in home runs? (*5 points*)

    A) 24 percent
    B) 34 percent
    C) 44 percent
    D) 54 percent

20. Who was the last player to win a Triple Crown in the National League? (*5 points*)

	4	5	6
VISITORS			
HOME			

4TH INNING

Top 4th

1. Name the all-time home run leader for these franchises that packed up and moved out of town.
(5 of 10: *6 points*; 8 of 10: *8 points*; 9 of 10: *9 points*; 10 of 10: *10 points*)

   a) St. Louis Browns
   b) Boston Braves
   c) Philadelphia Athletics
   d) Milwaukee Braves
   e) Brooklyn Dodgers
   f) New York Giants
   g) Washington Senators (who became the Minnesota Twins)
   h) Kansas City Athletics
   i) Seattle Pilots
   j) Washington Senators (who became the Texas Rangers)

2. Who has the fewest career wins among pitchers who have thrown a nine-inning perfect game? (*7 points*)

3. Mike Schmidt led the National League in homers eight times in his career. However, his second-highest single-season mark of 45, in 1979, did not lead the league. Who beat him out? (*4 points*)

4. Name the five players to have their uniform numbers retired by more than one team.
(4 of 5: *4 points*; 5 of 5: *5 points*)

5. This righthanded-hitting slugger hit 21 home runs one season without hitting a single homer off a lefty. Who is he? (*3 points*)

    A) Jeff Kent
    B) Matt Williams
    C) Ron Gant
    D) Albert Belle

6. The Giants had three Rookies of the Year in the 1950s. Who were they? (*5 points*)

7. Name the four players named Williams who have hit more than 200 home runs.
(3 of 4: *3 points*; 4 of 4: *5 points*)

8. Although only one major league franchise switched cities between 1972–98, the Milwaukee Brewers switched divisions four times in that span. Which of the following divisions have the Brewers *not* called home at some point? (*3 points*)

    A) AL East
    B) AL Central
    C) AL West
    D) NL West

9. What player went the longest between his first major league appearance and his second? (*5 points*)

10. What team won 101 games in 1961 and still finished eight games back in the standings? (*5 points*)

11. Which member of the Hall of Fame guided his team to the highest winning percentage in the 20th century in his first full season as a manager? (*4 points*)

    A) Hughie Jennings
    B) Earl Weaver
    C) Sparky Anderson
    D) Frank Chance

12. Who ranks second in homers among players whose last names begin with "H"? (*5 points*)

13. Who was the last player to lead his league in on-base percentage without reaching .400? (*5 points*)

    A) Tony Gwynn
    B) Pete Rose
    C) Carl Yastrzemski
    D) Terry Pendleton

14. Who was the oldest pitcher to start a World Series game? (*5 points*)

15. Who was the youngest pitcher to appear in a World Series game? (*5 points*)

16. The Orioles won the first 10 American League Championship Series games they played. Finally, on October 7, 1973, the Orioles were beaten in an ALCS contest. Which opposing pitcher ended their streak? (*4 points*)

    A) Ken Holtzman
    B) Vida Blue
    C) Catfish Hunter
    D) Jim Perry

17. Who holds the record for most stolen bases in a season without being caught? (*5 points*)

18. This Hall of Famer hit a home run in his first major league at bat and never homered again. (*6 points*)

19. In 1930 Lou Gehrig became the first player to have two seasons with 100 or more extra-base hits. Who was the first National League slugger to have two 100–extra-base-hit seasons? (*4 points*)

    A) Chuck Klein
    B) Ralph Kiner
    C) Mike Schmidt
    D) Mark McGwire

20. Who was the last pitcher to record 20 wins and 10 shutouts in a season? (*5 points*)

	4	5	6
VISITORS			
HOME			

Bottom 4th

1. Who was the first player to hit 50 homers and 50 doubles in the same season? (*4 points*)

2. Name the last team to score 20 or more runs in a World Series game. (*4 points*)

    A) 1997 Cleveland Indians
    B) 1931 Philadelphia Athletics
    C) 1927 New York Yankees
    D) None of the above

3. What manager had the most wins without ever winning a league championship? (*5 points*)

4. In 1947 Jackie Robinson was the first player to be named Rookie of the Year; two years later he was named Most Valuable Player, making him the first person to win both awards. Who was the first American League player to be named Rookie of the Year and Most Valuable Player? (*3 points*)

    A) Frank Robinson
    B) Fred Lynn
    C) Rod Carew
    D) Thurman Munson

5. Which pitcher holds the major league record for most consecutive batters retired (not necessarily in one game)? (*5 points*)

    A) Dennis Eckersley
    B) Sandy Koufax
    C) Orel Hershiser
    D) Jim Barr

6. Who holds the record for most RBIs in a World Series? (*5 points*)

    A) Bobby Richardson
    B) Babe Ruth
    C) Reggie Jackson
    D) George Brett

7. Who were the original five members of the Hall of Fame inducted in 1936? (4 of 5: *5 points*; 5 of 5: *6 points*)

8. Two pitchers share the record for most saves in a season past age 40. One of those pitchers is Dennis Eckersley, who at the age of 42 had 36 saves in 1997. Who is the other pitcher? (*5 points*)

9. When the Indians fired Mike Hargrove after the 1999 season, he was just seven wins shy of the club record for most career managerial victories. Who set that record? (*4 points*)

    A) Tris Speaker
    B) Lou Boudreau
    C) Al Lopez
    D) Napoleon Lajoie

10. Who served up Joe Carter's three-run blast that ended the 1993 Fall Classic? (*3 points*)

11. Since divisional play started in 1968, which is the only team to win 90 games and finish in fourth place? (*6 points*)

12. Name the two Hall of Fame pitchers who hold the career records for most wild pitches and most balks. (*5 points*)

13. Who had more stolen bases over a five-year span than any other player? (*5 points*)

14. Which of the athletes listed below did not play for both a major league baseball team and a National Football League team? (*4 points*)

    A) George Halas
    B) Cal Hubbard
    C) Ernie Nevers
    D) Brian Jordan

15. How many home dates did it take for the Rockies to break the 1 million mark in attendance in their inaugural season? (*3 points*)

    A) 17
    B) 27
    C) 37
    D) 47

16. When Sandy Koufax threw his fourth and final no-hitter against the Cubs in 1965, the Dodgers won the game, 1–0, with only one base hit   (the record for fewest hits in a game for two teams) . Who was the losing pitcher for the Cubs, and who got the one hit for Los Angeles? (1 of 2: *6 points*; 2 of 2: *8 points*)

17. Name the only player to win two batting titles for the Chicago Cubs. (*4 points*)

18. His nickname was "Buster," but can you come up with Cal McLish's much more colorful full given name? (*8 points*)

19. There are nine players whose last names begin with "M" who hit 40 homers in a season. Name them.   (5 of 9: *5 points*; 7 of 9: *7 points*; 8 of 9: *8 points*; 9 of 9: *10 points*)

20. In the history of postseason play, only a handful of teams have come back from three-games-to-one deficits to win a series. The Pirates did it in 1925 and 1979, but which team did it twice in one year?   (*3 points*)

    A) Kansas City Royals
    B) New York Yankees
    C) St. Louis Cardinals
    D) Washington Senators

5TH INNING

Top 5th

1. On September 20, 2000, this 12-year veteran set a record by making his first start after 603 career relief appearances. Who was this crafty lefthander? (*3 points*)

    A) Mike Stanton
    B) Chuck McElroy
    C) Gary Lavelle
    D) Jesse Orosco

2. During the Seattle Pilots' lone season in the American League, one pitcher led the team in both wins and losses. Who was he? (*6 points*)

3. Who holds the record for career pinch hits? (*4 points*)

    A) Lenny Harris
    B) Greg Gross
    C) Rusty Staub
    D) Manny Mota

4. What is the only position at which the Yankees have never had a Gold Glove winner? (*4 points*)

5. Excluding Yankees, what player has hit the most World Series home runs? (*6 points*)

6. On October 2, 1920, the Pittsburgh Pirates hosted the only tripleheader in the 20th century. Who were their guests on that very long day? (*5 points*)

    A) Chicago Cubs
    B) Cincinnati Reds
    C) New York Giants
    D) St. Louis Cardinals

7. There has been at least one 20-game winner in each season in major league history that wasn't shortened by a labor dispute, but in 1982 there was just one 20-game winner. Who was he? (*5 points*)

8. Between 1923–80 only four pitchers reached 3,000 career strikeouts, yet one batter was the milestone victim on two occasions. Which batter was twice a 3,000th-strikeout victim? (*5 points*)

    A) Steve O'Neill
    B) Frank Robinson
    C) Cesar Geronimo
    D) George Foster

9. In 1999 Houston closer Billy Wagner allowed a total of 14 runs in 66 appearances. He surrendered seven of those runs to one team. Which team was it? (*6 points*)

10. Who holds the Giants all-time record (New York and San Francisco) for career RBIs? (*4 points*)

11. Which future Hall of Fame manager made the last out of Johnny Vander Meer's second consecutive no-hitter in 1938? (*5 points*)

    A) Al Lopez
    B) Ernie Lombardi
    C) Leo Durocher
    D) Walter Alston

12. What is the record for most at bats in a major league game without a hit? (*6 points*)

13. Who took the loss in David Wells' perfect game? (*4 points*)

    A) Latroy Hawkins
    B) Ken Hill
    C) Brad Radke
    D) Eric Milton

14. In 1970 four different National League teams tied for the league lead in batting at .270. Two of those teams won division titles (Pirates and Reds), one finished second (Dodgers), and the other finished fifth. That team did, however, have the NL batting champion. Who was it and which team did he play for? (*6 points*)

15. What pitcher was voted onto the most All-Star teams? (*4 points*)

16. Who hit two home runs in two different World Series games in 1980? (*4 points*)

    A) Willie Aikens
    B) John Mayberry
    C) Mike Schmidt
    D) George Brett

17. Ty Cobb ranks first all-time in runs scored, with 2,246 runs. Among players whose last name begins with "C," who is second in runs? (*5 points*)

18. Who drove in the final run ever at Ebbets Field? (*5 points*)

    A) Duke Snider
    B) Junior Gilliam
    C) Roy Campanella
    D) Gil Hodges

19. What 20-game winner hit the most home runs in the same season? (*5 points*)

    A) Bob Gibson
    B) Wes Ferrell
    C) Earl Wilson
    D) Don Newcombe

20. What two members of the Hall of Fame hit homers in their last major league at bats? (*8 points*)

	4	**5**	**6**
VISITORS			
HOME			

Bottom 5th

1. Johnny Vander Meer made baseball history in 1938 when he pitched consecutive no-hitters. Nine times in baseball history pitchers have thrown consecutive one-hitters. Who did it most recently? (*4 points*)

    A) Greg Maddux
    B) Dave Stieb
    C) Steve Carlton
    D) Randy Johnson

2. Name the seven players who have won three MVP Awards. (4 of 7: *6 points*; 6 of 7: *7 points*; 7 of 7: *8 points*)

3. Baseball games are played until there is a winner, but weather and darkness (in stadiums without lights) resulted in many ties over the years. Through the 2000 season, however, there had only been three games that ended in ties in World Series play. When was the last one? (*5 points*)

    A) 1907
    B) 1912
    C) 1922
    D) 1996

4. What BYU star quit the Toronto Blue Jays to join the Boston Celtics? (*3 points*)

5. Who was the oldest player to steal a base? (*5 points*)

6. Which of these players was in the top three in walks drawn in the 1990s? (*4 points*)

    A) Rickey Henderson
    B) Jeff Bagwell
    C) Tony Phillips
    D) Mark McGwire

7. In Ron Guidry's superb 25–3 season, all of his losses came at the hands of pitchers named Mike. Name the three pitchers. (2 of 3: *4 points*; 3 of 3: *6 points*)

8. What were the most home runs Hall of Famer Frank "Home Run" Baker ever hit in a season? (*5 points*)

    A) 12
    B) 26
    C) 16
    D) 19

9. Who tossed the first no-hitter in National League history, in 1876? (*5 points*)

    A) Tommy Bond
    B) Tommy John
    C) George Bradley
    D) Kid Nichols

10. What major league franchises were the first to draw 1 million, 2 million, 3 million, and 4 million spectators in a season, and in which years were the plateaus reached? (3 of 4: *4 points*; 4 of 4: *6 points*)

11. The Minnesota world championship teams of 1987 and 1991 had four everyday position players in common. Who were they? (3 of 4: *4 points*; 4 of 4: *6 points*)

12. The Pittsburgh Pirates and Boston Pilgrims combined to hit three home runs in the first two World Series games ever played in 1903. When was the next home run hit in World Series play? (*5 points*)

A) 1904
B) 1906
C) 1908
D) 1910

13. This pitcher won *The Sporting News* AL Rookie Pitcher of the Year award in 1961—and never pitched again. Who was he? (*6 points*)

14. As of 2001, six players have hit 50 or more homers in a season without winning the home run title. Name them. (4 of 6: *4 points*; 5 of 6: *5 points*; 6 of 6: *6 points*)

15. The spitball was officially banned in 1920, but 17 pitchers were allowed to continue to use it in the major leagues. Who threw the last "legal" spitter? (*5 points*)

A) Jesse Haines
B) Burleigh Grimes
C) Eddie Cicotte
D) Gaylord Perry

16. On September 16, 1996, Paul Molitor became the 21st member of the 3,000-hit club. What did he do that no other member of this exclusive club had done? (*4 points*)

A) Homer for his 3,000th hit
B) Triple for his 3,000th hit
C) The youngest player to reach 3,000 hits
D) The first Twin to do it

17. Who was the first player to hit four homers in a World Series? (*4 points*)

    A) Lou Gehrig
    B) Goose Goslin
    C) Babe Ruth
    D) Aaron Ward

18. Name the top two players in career home runs whose last names begin with "Z." (*4 points*)

19. The National League had been in existence for 70 years before the first playoff was required to break a tie for first place at the end of a season. Which team won that first historic playoff? (*4 points*)

    A) St. Louis Cardinals
    B) Chicago Cubs
    C) Brooklyn Dodgers
    D) New York Giants

20. What is the only father-son combination in the Baseball Hall of Fame? (*5 points*)

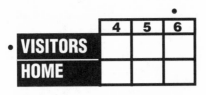

6TH INNING

Top 6th

1. Of the original 16 teams from 1901, which is the only one that hasn't sent an outfielder to the Hall of Fame? (*5 points*)

2. Fielding wizard Ozzie Smith was an automatic Gold Glove at shortstop, winning the award each year from 1980–92. Which National League shortstop broke his hold on the award in 1993? (*4 points*)

    A) Jay Bell
    B) Barry Larkin
    C) Royce Clayton
    D) Rey Ordonez

3. Only two teams since 1910 have won World Series without hitting a home run. Name them. (*7 points*)

4. Which infielder played on seven NL East champions in the 1970s? (*5 points*)

    A) Richie Hebner
    B) Bob Robertson
    C) Dave Cash
    D) Pete Rose

5. Which one of these Hall of Famers never led the league in a single offensive category? (*4 points*)

    A) Joe Kelley
    B) George Kelly
    C) George Kell
    D) Rabbit Maranville

6. Only two players in modern baseball history have had more than 700 at bats in a season. Name them. (*5 points*)

7. Who has won the most Cy Young Awards without ever winning more than 20 games in a season? (*6 points*)

8. Bob Gibson went 3–0 with a 1.00 ERA in the Cardinals' 1967 World Series win over the Red Sox. Who had the other victory for the Cards in that Series? (*5 points*)

    A) Roger Craig
    B) Steve Carlton
    C) Nellie Briles
    D) Hal Woodeshick

9. What is the latest inning in which a home run has been hit in major league history, and who hit it? (*6 points*)

10. In 1997 Randy Johnson became the first pitcher to strike out 19 batters twice in one season. Against which teams did he turn the trick? (*5 points*)

    A) Baltimore and Cleveland
    B) Oakland and Chicago White Sox
    C) New York Yankees and Colorado
    D) Detroit and Houston

11. Who was the first player in the 20th century to hit 20 home runs in a season? (*5 points*)

A) Honus Wagner
B) Frank Schulte
C) Gavvy Cravath
D) Babe Ruth

12. What manager took four different clubs to the post-season? (*5 points*)

13. Excluding Colorado, Florida, and Tampa Bay, which is the only major league franchise that has not had a Cy Young Award winner? (*4 points*)

14. From 1985–87 Vince Coleman stole 326 bases, topping 100 steals and leading the National League each year. Which National Leaguer had the second-highest total over that three-year span? (*4 points*)

15. Who was the first major league player to have his uniform number retired? (*5 points*)

16. Who led American League first basemen in errors in 1999? (*5 points*)

A) Carlos Delgado
B) Tino Martinez
C) Ron Coomer
D) Tony Clark

17. Which of these Hall of Famers was the only one to see action in a World Series? (*5 points*)

A) Elmer Flick
B) Luke Appling
C) Heinie Manush
D) George Kell

18. What three teammates played together for 15 seasons—the longest combined tour of duty of any trio in major league history? (*7 points*)

19. From the first year of the Gold Glove, 1957, through the 2000 season, pitchers who have won the award have tended to win it multiple times—especially in the American League. In those 43 seasons, just three AL pitchers won the Gold Glove one time only. Which of the following pitchers won just one Gold Glove Award? (*4 points*)

    A) Bobby Shantz
    B) Jim Kaat
    C) Mark Langston
    D) Bret Saberhagen

20. Name the three players to win a Triple Crown after 1950. (*4 points*)

	4	5	6
VISITORS			
HOME			

Bottom 6th

1. Mark McGwire recently became the all-time home run leader for players with last names beginning with "Mc." Who are the other three "Mc" players with at least 200 career home runs? (2 of 3: *5 points*; 3 of 3: *7 points*)

2. Which player hit seven home runs over two consecutive World Series? (*4 points*)

    A) Babe Ruth
    B) Duke Snider
    C) Reggie Jackson
    D) Mickey Mantle

3. Which player hit nine home runs over three consecutive World Series? (*4 points*)

    A) Lou Gehrig
    B) Reggie Jackson
    C) Babe Ruth
    D) Mickey Mantle

4. Bert Blyleven notched more strikeouts (3,701) than several Hall of Fame pitchers, including Tom Seaver, Walter Johnson, Fergie Jenkins, and Bob Gibson. How many times did Blyleven lead his league in strikeouts? (*5 points*)

5. Ralph Kiner won the National League home run title seven straight years, from his rookie year of 1946 through 1952, his last full season in Pittsburgh. Who broke Kiner's string in '53? (*5 points*)

6. Who of the following did *not* manage the California Angels in 1994? (*4 points*)

    A) Buck Rodgers
    B) John Wathan
    C) Rene Lachemann
    D) Bobby Knoop

7. What Hall of Famer took his final major league swings during the 1973 World Series? (*4 points*)

8. Which was the first major league team to win 100 games in a season? (*5 points*)

    A) Boston Beaneaters
    B) Chicago Cubs
    C) New York Yankees
    D) Brooklyn Superbas

9. What team first drafted Roger Clemens? (*6 points*)

10. Among players whose last names begin with "B," who are first and second all-time in homers? (*5 points*)

11. Which team won a National League pennant with a record-low .509 winning percentage? (*5 points*)

12. "Sure, nice guys can win—if they're nice guys with a lot of talent. Nice guys with a little talent finish fourth, and nice guys with no talent finish last." Who uttered this quote? (*5 points*)

    A) Casey Stengel
    B) Tom Seaver
    C) Mickey Mantle
    D) Sandy Koufax

13. Name the only player in major league history to play all 162 of his team's games in the field and not commit an error. (*5 points*)

    A) Rocky Colavito
    B) Darren Lewis
    C) Gary Pettis
    D) Ryne Sandberg

14. In 2000 the Cincinnati Reds became the second franchise in modern major league history to go through an entire season without being shut out. Name the first team to score at least a run in every game in a season. (*7 points*)

15. Only once did a lefthanded batter lead the National League in home runs in the 1980s. Who was it, and in what season? (*5 points*)

16. Which of these players was the first major league pitcher to hit three home runs in a game? (*5 points*)

    A) Deacon Phillippe
    B) Babe Ruth
    C) Wes Ferrell
    D) Guy Hecker

17. How many players have won the Gold Glove Award at more than one position? (*4 points*)

18. Who was the last pitcher to record a 3–0 record in a World Series? (*5 points*)

    A) Sandy Koufax
    B) Bob Gibson
    C) Duane Ward
    D) Mickey Lolich

19. Who was the last pitcher to record an 0–3 record in a World Series? (*5 points*)

    A) Tom Seaver
    B) George Frazier
    C) Mitch Williams
    D) Bob Stanley

20. On May 3, 1980, a rare triple steal was pulled off against the Detroit Tigers. What team engineered the feat? (*5 points*)

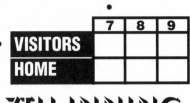

7TH INNING

Top 7th

1. Who played for all three 100-loss teams in 1985? (*4 points*)

    A) Pat Tabler
    B) Joel Youngblood
    C) Jim Morrison
    D) Johnnie LeMaster

2. In addition to being the only "Subway Series" west of the Mississippi, the 1944 World Series between the St. Louis Cardinals and St. Louis Browns was noteworthy for something it lacked. What did not occur in the 1944 World Series that has occurred in every other one before or since? (*5 points*)

3. One of Ted Williams' most famous home runs came in the 1946 All-Star Game when he homered off a lobbed, high-arced toss known as the "eephus pitch." Which National Leaguer threw the gopher ball? (*4 points*)

    A) Rip Sewell
    B) Claude Passeau
    C) Bob Feller
    D) Warren Spahn

4. Who led the American League in hitting in the strike-shortened 1994 season? (*4 points*)

5. Who won three Cy Young Awards without anyone else getting a single vote? (*4 points*)

6. Who started and won the first regular-season game played by the Yankees at Shea Stadium? (*4 points*)

    A) Hideki Irabu
    B) Ramiro Mendoza
    C) Andy Pettitte
    D) Mel Stottlemyre

7. How many best-of-nine World Series sweeps have there been? (*6 points*)

8. Who was the last pitcher to steal five or more bases in a season? (*5 points*)

    A) Bob Gibson
    B) Mike Hampton
    C) Joaquin Andujar
    D) Rick Ankiel

9. What pitcher had a record 10 complete games in the World Series? (*6 points*)

10. Of the following Hall of Famers, which one never hit 30 or more home runs in a season? (*4 points*)

    A) Mel Ott
    B) Al Kaline
    C) Jim Bottomley
    D) Earl Averill

11. On August 4, 1982, Joel Youngblood became the first player to get hits for two different teams in two different cities in one day. Youngblood started the day as a member of the New York Mets, but what team did he finish the day with? (*4 points*)

   A) Montreal Expos
   B) Chicago Cubs
   C) Philadelphia Phillies
   D) New York Yankees

12. Which major league pitcher set a 20th century record with a .433 batting average over a full season? (*6 points*)

   A) Rick Camp
   B) Walter Johnson
   C) Jack Bentley
   D) Bob Lemon

13. Which of the following teams did *not* have its starting outfield enshrined in the Hall of Fame? (*5 points*)

   A) 1924 Detroit Tigers
   B) 1927 New York Yankees
   C) 1926 Pittsburgh Pirates
   D) 1927 Washington Senators

14. Among players whose last names begin with "Y," who are first, second, and third in all-time home runs?
(2 of 3: *5 points*; 3 of 3: *7 points*)

15. Who holds the single-season record for innings pitched, post-1920? (*6 points*)

16. A National League tradition stretching back more than a century ended in 1995 when the first "non-champion" participated in the postseason. Which was the first NL team to be crowned "Wild Card" champion? (*4 points*)

A) Colorado Rockies
B) Los Angeles Dodgers
C) Atlanta Braves
D) Houston Astros

17. Three players have been named World Series MVP more than once. Who are they? (2 of 3: *5 points*; 3 of 3: *7 points*)

18. Which of the following players won back-to-back American League batting titles in the 1950s? (*5 points*)

A) Mickey Mantle
B) Al Kaline
C) Ferris Fain
D) Ted Williams

19. Who started in right field for the Pirates in their first regular-season game after Hall of Fame right fielder Roberto Clemente was killed in a plane crash? (*5 points*)

A) Richie Zisk
B) Richie Hebner
C) Dave Parker
D) Manny Sanguillen

20. What pitcher won the Cy Young Award despite posting a losing record? (*5 points*)

	7	8	9
VISITORS			
HOME			

Bottom 7th

1. Which pitcher holds the record for lifetime winning percentage? (*3 points*)

    A) Whitey Ford
    B) Dave Foutz
    C) Mike Mussina
    D) Lefty Grove

2. Who led all shortstops in on-base plus slugging (OPS) in 2000? (*5 points*)

3. Who hit the first World Series home run in Yankee Stadium? (*5 points*)

    A) Babe Ruth
    B) Lou Gehrig
    C) Wally Pipp
    D) Casey Stengel

4. Since Jackie Robinson stole home for the Brooklyn Dodgers in the 1955 World Series, only one other player has accomplished the feat. Who was he? (*7 points*)

5. What was the only decade of the 20th century in which a team from Pennsylvania never reached the World Series? (*4 points*)

6. The world champion Reds led the major leagues with 50 saves in 1975. Who led the Reds and the NL in saves that year? (*4 points*)

    A) Rawly Eastwick
    B) Clay Carroll
    C) Pedro Borbon
    D) Will McEnaney

7. John Wathan stole 36 bases in 1982, setting the major league record for thefts by a catcher. Whose record did Wathan break? (*6 points*)

8. How many World Series sweeps have the Yankees enjoyed? (*5 points*)

    A) Nine
    B) Six
    C) Eight
    D) Five

9. Of the following Hall of Fame pitchers, which one enjoyed the fewest 20-win seasons? (*5 points*)

    A) Don Sutton
    B) Dazzy Vance
    C) Candy Cummings
    D) Jesse Haines

10. After Willie Mays led the league in stolen bases from 1956–59, this player led the National League in thefts in 1960. (*4 points*)

11. Which pitcher retired 32 batters in a row and then singled in the winning run in the 12th inning on September 18, 1971? (*5 points*)

A) Dock Ellis
B) Rick Wise
C) Steve Carlton
D) Tom Seaver

12. Kansas City first baseman Mike Sweeney finished the 2000 season with 29 home runs and 144 RBIs. Who was the last player to drive in that many runs without hitting 30 homers? (*6 points*)

A) Lou Gehrig
B) Tommy Davis
C) Chili Davis
D) Al Simmons

13. Who had the most hits and made the final out in the 1986 World Series? (*6 points*)

14. Who has the most Gold Glove Awards among players not in the Hall of Fame? (*3 points*)

15. Christy Mathewson's younger brother Henry made three career pitching appearances, all with the New York Giants. How many batters did he walk in his lone career start? (*7 points*)

16. On September 26, 2000, Omar Daal won his final start of the year to keep him from becoming the first pitcher since Brian Kingman in 1980 to lose 20 games in a season. Kingman went 8–20 for the Oakland A's that year, but who was the last National League pitcher to lose 20 games? (*5 points*)

A) Steve Carlton
B) Phil Niekro
C) Jerry Koosman
D) Anthony Young

17. Who holds the modern record for walks surrendered in a season? (*5 points*)

    A) Nolan Ryan
    B) Randy Johnson
    C) Bob Feller
    D) Bobo Newsom

18. Three players have hit 400 home runs in a decade (e.g. 1970–79). Who are they? (2 of 3: *3 points*; 3 of 3: *5 points*)

19. Who was the first player to homer in Canada in both leagues? (*5 points*)

    A) Rusty Staub
    B) Richie Zisk
    C) Ron Fairly
    D) Otto Velez

20. Among players whose last name begins with "F," who is second in home runs? (*5 points*)

8TH INNING

Top 8th

1. When the Brooklyn Dodgers won the World Series in 1955, the club tied a record for most starters used in a Series. How many different starters did manager Walter Alston employ? (*3 points*)

2. For which pennant winner did Tom Seaver throw his last pitch? (*4 points*)

    A) Cincinnati Reds
    B) Chicago White Sox
    C) Boston Red Sox
    D) New York Mets

3. Who is the first American Leaguer in the 20th century, other than Babe Ruth, to hit 30 home runs in a season? (*6 points*)

4. "The Mendoza Line" isn't near the equator—it's located at the .200 batting average level. Light-hitting Mario Mendoza is the man who inspired this handle, but what was his actual lifetime batting average? (*5 points*)

    A) .188
    B) .201
    C) .215
    D) .250

5. Who was the first player to have two four-hit games in one World Series? (*5 points*)

    A) Yogi Berra
    B) Mickey Mantle
    C) Robin Yount
    D) Paul Molitor

6. Who was the last Boston player to win a home run title? (*5 points*)

7. With a minimum of 1,000 innings pitched, there were three pitchers to post ERAs under 3.00 for the 1990s. Name them. (2 of 3: *5 points*; 3 of 3: *7 points*)

8. Which outfielder holds the single-season record for participating in double plays? (*5 points*)

    A) Roberto Clemente
    B) Willie Mays
    C) Mel Ott
    D) Bo Jackson

9. Name the first father-and-son tandem to win All-Star Game MVP awards. (*4 points*)

10. Which pitcher won the most 1–0 games during the 20th century? (*5 points*)

A) Lefty Grove
B) Hoyt Wilhelm
C) Grover Alexander
D) Walter Johnson

11. Who were the Giants' baserunners when Bobby Thomson hit the "Shot Heard 'Round the World" to win the 1951 pennant? (*5 points*)

A) Al Dark and Don Mueller
B) Whitey Lockman and Don Mueller
C) Don Mueller and Clint Hartung
D) Clint Hartung and Whitey Lockman

12. What pitcher lost the most games in a season he won the Cy Young Award? (*6 points*)

13. What former prison inmate led the AL in stolen bases in 1978 and 1980? (*4 points*)

14. Who is the youngest pitcher to record a complete-game shutout in the World Series? (*6 points*)

15. Leo Durocher managed four different teams in his career. Name them. (*5 points*)

16. Who was the first Met to homer at Yankee Stadium in a regular-season game? (*4 points*)

A) John Olerud
B) Edgardo Alfonzo
C) Bernard Gilkey
D) Mike Piazza

17. Which expansion team paid the smallest fee to enter the major leagues? (*4 points*)

    A) Los Angeles Angels
    B) Washington Senators
    C) New York Mets
    D) Houston Colt .45s

18. Name the eight position players elected to the Hall of Fame who never had a major league season in which they either scored or drove in 100 or more runs. (3 of 8: *3 points*; 5 of 8: *5 points*; 7 of 8: *7 points*; 8 of 8: *9 points*)

19. Who managed in the World Series with three different teams from the same league? (*4 points*)

    A) Sparky Anderson
    B) Alvin Dark
    C) Bill McKechnie
    D) Dick Williams

20. Who was the first pitcher to throw a no-hitter and later save 40 games in a season? (*4 points*)

	7	8	9
VISITORS			
HOME			

Bottom 8th

1. Among players whose last names begin with "V," who are first and second all-time in home runs? (*6 points*)

2. After "Iron Men" Cal Ripken Jr. and Lou Gehrig, who is third on the all-time list of consecutive games played? (*5 points*)

    A) Joe Sewell
    B) Nellie Fox
    C) Billy Williams
    D) Everett Scott

3. From 1979–82, the Dodgers had four consecutive Rookies of the Year. Who were they? (3 of 4: *3 points*; 4 of 4: *5 points*)

4. Who pitched a record 27 scoreless innings in one World Series? (*4 points*)

    A) Bob Gibson
    B) Jack Morris
    C) Tom Glavine
    D) Christy Mathewson

5. Who holds the record for most at bats in a season without hitting a home run? (*5 points*)

    A) Ozzie Smith
    B) Rafael Belliard
    C) Heinie Groh
    D) Rabbit Maranville

6. Roger Maris beat out the same person twice to win the American League MVP in 1960 and 1961. Who was the runner-up? (*4 points*)

7. Name the last trio of teammates to finish 1-2-3 in a batting race. (*6 points*)

8. Which of these players was baseball's leading RBI man of the 1980s? (*4 points*)

    A) Mike Schmidt
    B) Eddie Murray
    C) Dave Winfield
    D) Dale Murphy

9. In 1912 I finished the season with 35 complete games, 10 shutouts, and a 34–5 record; I then went on to win three World Series games. Who am I? (*6 points*)

10. Which of the following Hall of Famers never played in an All-Star Game? (*4 points*)

    A) Monte Irvin
    B) Ernie Lombardi
    C) Chick Hafey
    D) Larry Doby

11. In 1970 Willie Stargell hit the first home run at Three Rivers Stadium. In 2000 he was on hand for the last homer at Three Rivers. Who hit the final home run at the stadium? (*5 points*)

  A) Jason Kendall
  B) Adrian Brown
  C) Sammy Sosa
  D) John Wehner

12. On July 24, 1968, Hoyt Wilhelm pitched in his 907th major league game, breaking Cy Young's record for most pitching appearances in a career. Later that year, another pitcher equaled Walter Johnson's record of 802 pitching appearances for one team, but was traded before he could break it. Name him. (*6 points*)

13. Name two of the three players who hit .400 or better in 1922. (*5 points*)

14. Only two pitching staffs in the 20th century were able to boast a quartet of 20-game winners. Name the teams and the seasons. (*6 points*)

15. Which lefthanded batter hit four consecutive homers in a game? (*5 points*)

  A) Bobby Murcer
  B) Ted Williams
  C) Lou Gehrig
  D) Babe Ruth

16. Who was the first player in major league history to bat in 1,000 games as a designated hitter and play 1,000 games at another position? (*4 points*)

  A) Paul Molitor
  B) Harold Baines
  C) Dave Winfield
  D) Hal McRae

17. No Hall of Famer has ever made an unassisted triple play, but two Hall of Famers have hit into one. Who are they? (*5 points*)

    A) Roberto Clemente and Robin Yount
    B) Jim Bottomley and Paul Waner
    C) Don Sutton and Mike Schmidt
    D) Babe Ruth and Lou Gehrig

18. Since the introduction of the MVP Award in the early 1920s, there have been nine Triple Crown seasons. How many times did the Triple Crown winner fail to win that season's MVP Award? (*6 points*)

19. Which catcher for a last-place team led his league in RBIs in 1992? (*4 points*)

    A) Mike Piazza
    B) Darren Daulton
    C) Ivan Rodriguez
    D) B.J. Surhoff

20. Who hit more home runs as a third baseman than anyone in American League history? (*5 points*)

	7	8	9
VISITORS			
HOME			

9TH INNING

Top 9th

1. Name the only major leaguer to place in a national drag racing championship. (*7 points*)

2. Which pitcher won seven consecutive World Series games? (*5 points*)

    A) Whitey Ford
    B) Bob Gibson
    C) Lefty Gomez
    D) Herb Pennock

3. What two Hall of Famers were traded for each other in 1930? (*6 points*)

4. Which one of these teams had three of its four starting infielders elected to the Hall of Fame? (*5 points*)

    A) 1902 Chicago Cubs
    B) 1894 Baltimore Orioles
    C) 1898 Cincinnati Reds
    D) 1922 Pittsburgh Pirates

5. Who holds the record for most consecutive seasons of both scoring and driving in 100 or more runs? (4 points)

    A) Lou Gehrig
    B) Babe Ruth
    C) Jimmie Foxx
    D) Hank Aaron

6. What was the Yankees' combined postseason record in 1998 and 1999? (*5 points*)

7. What two players (both pitchers) were elected to the Hall of Fame with the highest percentage of votes? (*6 points*)

8. The first World Series game played on artificial turf took place on October 10, 1970. What city hosted the game? (*4 points*)

    A) Pittsburgh
    B) Cincinnati
    C) St. Louis
    D) Philadelphia

9. Name the only All-American basketball player to win a Most Valuable Player Award. (*6 points*)

10. Which pitcher had the most winning seasons in the major leagues? (*4 points*)

    A) Cy Young
    B) Warren Spahn
    C) Grover Alexander
    D) Nolan Ryan

11. Who was the last pitcher to surrender a home run to Hank Aaron? (*5 points*)

    A) Al Downing
    B) Dick Drago
    C) Jerry Augustine
    D) Jack Billingham

12. What infielder shares the National League record of eight batting titles? (*4 points*)

13. Name the three players who were selected for 20 All-Star Games. (*5 points*)

14. Name the only member of the Baseball Hall of Fame who also served as a member of the U.S. Senate. (*5 points*)

15. Who was the first player to hit grand slams in consecutive games? (*5 points*)

    A) Jimmy Bannon
    B) Lou Gehrig
    C) Don Mattingly
    D) Stan Musial

16. Whose game-winning hit in extra innings clinched the 1978 NL pennant? (*5 points*)

    A) Bill Russell
    B) Ron Cey
    C) Davey Lopes
    D) Garry Maddox

17. Who is the only player to win a Triple Crown, the Rookie of the Year Award, and be inducted into the Hall of Fame? (*4 points*)

18. I won 198 National League games in the 1930s and '40s, but played three seasons at third base before throwing my first major league pitch. Who am I? (*6 points*)

19. What outfielder played in his first and last World Series 19 years apart? (*5 points*)

20. Which player could have tied Babe Ruth's single-season home run record in 1932 if rainouts hadn't erased two homers? (*4 points*)

    A) Hank Greenberg
    B) Hack Wilson
    C) Lou Gehrig
    D) Jimmie Foxx

	7	8	9
VISITORS			
HOME			

Bottom 9th

1. Who was the first member of the Milwaukee Brewers to win an MVP Award? (*3 points*)

    A) Pete Vuckovich
    B) Rollie Fingers
    C) Robin Yount
    D) Hank Aaron

2. What letter begins the most last names of players who hit more than 400 home runs? (*4 points*)

3. Who was the first player in American League history to hit three home runs in one game? (*5 points*)

    A) Babe Ruth
    B) Ty Cobb
    C) Ken Williams
    D) George Sisler

4. Who holds the major league record for most pinch-hit home runs in a season? (*5 points*)

5. In the 1934 All-Star Game, Carl Hubbell struck out Babe Ruth, Lou Gehrig, Jimmie Foxx, Al Simmons, and Joe Cronin in succession. Who was the American League batter who ended Hubbell's string of strikeouts? (*6 points*)

6. Which Atlanta Braves pitcher struck out Pete Rose to end his 44-game hitting streak in 1978? (*5 points*)

  A) Phil Niekro
  B) Andy Messersmith
  C) Gene Garber
  D) Larry McWilliams

7. In 1927 the New York Yankees swept the Pittsburgh Pirates in the World Series. How many future Hall of Famers participated in those four games? (*5 points*)

8. Name the only man in major league history to homer in both his first and his final plate appearances. (*7 points*)

9. Who was the first major league pitcher to throw a no-hitter and hit a homer on the same day? (*7 points*)

10. In 1930 this club finished last in the National League despite a team batting average of .315. Who were they? (*5 points*)

11. What player had the most seasons in which he homered more often than he struck out? (*5 points*)

12. Who was the only pitcher to win three consecutive Triple Crowns—wins, strikeouts, and ERA—in the 20th century? (*4 points*)

13. What player holds club records for highest single-season batting average with three separate teams? (*5 points*)

14. Who was the first hitter to have a .300 batting average, 30 homers, and 100 RBIs in a season? (*4 points*)

15. What big league pitcher holds the record for most wins without a loss in a season? (*6 points*)

16. Who had the only 40 homer/.400 batting average season in baseball history?   (*5 points*)

17. Who is the only player since 1900 to drive in 100 or more runs in a season without hitting a home run?   (*5 points*)

    A) Tommy Herr
    B) Eddie Collins
    C) Lave Cross
    D) Bill Sweeney

18. Post–World War II, what player accumulated the highest RBI total in one season without hitting a home run?
(*5 points*)

19. Who led the National League in RBIs with the lowest season total?   (*5 points*)

    A) Will Clark
    B) Heinie Zimmerman
    C) Sherry Magee
    D) Hi Myers

20. Who was the only player ever to be traded after winning the Triple Crown?   (*4 points*)

ANSWERS

Top 1st

1. 1B Jimmie Foxx, Frank Thomas / 2B Joe Morgan / SS Ernie Banks / 3B Mike Schmidt / C Yogi Berra / LF Barry Bonds / CF Mickey Mantle, Dale Murphy / RF Roger Maris / P Hal Newhouser   (5 of 11: *3 points*; 7 of 11: *4 points*; 9 of 11: *7 points*; 11 of 11: *9 points*)

The only non-Hall of Famers in the group are Thomas, Bonds, Murphy, and Maris. Bonds is a lock for Cooperstown, and with a few more big years, Thomas will be able to say the same.

2. Darryl Strawberry and Jose Vizcaino   (*4 points*)

Straw's tenure with the Mets was from 1983–90, he was a Dodger for the next three seasons, a Giant in 1994, and finally a Yankee from 1995–2000. Vizcaino debuted with the Dodgers in 1989, played for the Mets from 1994–96, spent a year with the Giants in 1997, and was wearing pinstripes in 2000.

3. Dick Littlefield and $30,000   (*6 points*)

Pitcher Dick Littlefield played for 10 teams in nine seasons, compiling a 33–54 record; Robinson played his entire major league career in Brooklyn.

4. Nomar Garciaparra and Vladimir Guerrero (*4 points*)

Nomar (who did it in 1997) and Vlad (1999) are in pretty select company. The other two players to accomplish the feat are Rogers Hornsby and Joe DiMaggio.

5. A) Mordecai Brown (*4 points*)

Matty and Cubs pitcher Mordecai "Three Finger" Brown both closed out their careers in the same game on September 4, 1916. The Labor Day game, specially arranged to attract a large crowd, was won by Mathewson's Reds, 10–8. It was the only game that Mathewson, traded in the middle of the 1916 season to manage Cincinnati, did not pitch in a New York Giants uniform.

6. D) David Justice (*3 points*)

In 2000 David Justice hit 21 homers with the Indians and, following a trade on June 29, hit 20 more with the Yankees. Fred McGriff, who helped spark the Braves to a division title in 1993, hit 19 homers for Atlanta after smacking 18 for the Padres.

7. Mike Marshall (*4 points*)

Mike Marshall won a National League Cy Young Award in 1974, his first year with the Dodgers. He appeared in 106 games that year, won 15, and threw 208⅓ innings, exclusively in relief.

8. Sam Crawford (*5 points*)

Sam Crawford hit 16 for Cincinnati in 1901 and seven for Detroit in 1908. A Hall of Famer and teammate of Ty Cobb, Crawford was one of the best players of the dead-ball era. His year-by-year triples totals look like someone's doubles totals—he hit a record 309 triples in 19 seasons.

9. Keith McDonald (*4 points*)

Keith McDonald of the St. Louis Cardinals became the second player in history to homer in his first two big league at bats on July 6, 2000. The only other player to accomplish the feat was Bob Nieman of the St. Louis Browns in 1951.

10. Eddie Mathews, Hank Aaron, Joe Adcock, and Frank Thomas (3 of 4: *5 points*; 4 of 4: *7 points*)

Mathews is a member of the 500-homer club, Aaron is baseball's home run king, and Adcock and Thomas both rank in the top 100 in career home runs.

11. Eddie Stanky (*8 points*)

Eddie Stanky drew 137 walks for Brooklyn in 1946 without hitting a single homer. "Muggsy" hit just 29 homers in 1,259 career games, but he had an incredible eye at the plate. He drew more than 100 walks in a season six times—twice topping 140.

12. Japan, Mexico, South Korea, the Dominican Republic, and the United States   (4 of 5: *4 points*; 5 of 5: *5 points*)

Hideo Nomo, Ismael Valdes, Chan Ho Park, Pedro Astacio, and Tom Candiotti convened to lead the National League in strikeouts and opponents' batting average.

13. The Teens (*4 points*)

The 1919 "Black Sox" Series was expanded to the best of nine in the exuberance which followed the end of World War I, and Cincinnati won it in eight games. The 1912 Series between Boston and the New York Giants was a best-of-seven Series that went the distance; but Game 2 was called on account of darkness after 11 innings with the score tied 6–6, so—technically—it took eight games to decide the Series.

14. D) Manny Alexander   (3 points)

Second baseman Manny Alexander played second base the night Cal Ripken set the major league record with his 2,131st consecutive game. The following year Alexander snapped Ripken's streak of 2,216 consecutive games at shortstop when manager Davey Johnson shifted Cal to third base.

15. Darrell Evans and Dwight Evans   (*6 points*)

Darrell hit 414 homers in his career, Dwight 385. No. 3 on this list is way down to Del Ennis, who hit 288.

16. Luis Aparicio   (*4 points*)

Aparicio led the American League in stolen bases nine consecutive seasons, 1956–64. He also put together a string of seven straight All-Star selections from 1958–64.

17. Dazzy Vance   (*3 points*)

As a child, Vance had a neighbor who owned a rifle of which he was inordinately proud. Whenever the neighbor showed it off, he'd say, "Ain't it a dazzy?" Vance took a liking to the expression and soon his schoolmates hung the nickname on him for good. He was inducted into the Hall of Fame in 1955, 20 years after he retired.

18. 1992 Chicago White Sox   (*7 points*)

Roberto Hernandez saved 12 games in his first full season, lefty Scott Radinsky saved 15, and single-season record holder Bobby Thigpen saved 22 in 1992. The trio of relievers finished two saves behind AL MVP and Cy Young Award winner Dennis Eckersley.

19. B) Kansas City Athletics (*4 points*)

In 1961 the Kansas City A's finished in the American League basement with the new Washington Senators. The 1961 season was the first with that many teams in a major league since the National League reduced from 12 teams to eight after the 1899 season. The AL added the Senators and Los Angeles Angels as expansion teams in 1961.

20. Seals Stadium (*6 points*)

Seals Stadium in San Francisco was the site for the first-ever major league game in California on April 15, 1958. Ruben Gomez and the Giants beat the Dodgers, 8–0.

Bottom 1st

1. Robin Yount (*5 points*)

Robin Yount joined the Brewers in 1974 at the age of 18, and had no less than 454 at bats (excepting 1981) over his next 19 seasons in Milwaukee, 1975–93. Yount holds franchise career records for runs, hits, doubles, triples, home runs, and RBIs.

2. General William D. Eckert (*4 points*)

Eckert was a surprise pick for baseball's fourth commissioner on November 17, 1965. Although only in office for three seasons, Eckert made great strides in improving the business side of the game. With a Master's Degree from the Harvard Graduate School of Business Administration, Eckert streamlined business methods and gave franchises more stable foundations with bigger stadiums and longer leases.

3. B) Four days rest   (*2 points*)

National League starters had a 4.53 ERA when they pitched on four days rest in 1999, compared with 4.72 for five days rest. The highest ERA for these situations was pitching on six or more days rest (4.98).

4. Vic Raschi   (*5 points*)

Vic Raschi of the New York Yankees won the clincher in both the 1949 and 1951 Series, and won Game 6 to tie the 1952 Series before relieving the next day in victorious Game 7.

5. Four   (*6 points*)

Bagwell hit four home runs in 481 at bats. His first four years in the majors with Houston he hit 15, 18, 20, and 39 homers.

6. C) Federal League   (*3 points*)

The Federal League existed as a major league from 1914–15 and attracted several of the game's biggest stars. The FL filed a lawsuit against organized baseball, claiming that the existing leagues were an illegal trust. Kenesaw Mountain Landis, at the time a federal court judge in Chicago, stalled his decision and the FL eventually had little choice but to sign a peace treaty that disbanded the league and gave its owners a $600,000 settlement.

7. 1980 Oakland Athletics   (*6 points*)

The 1980 Oakland A's, managed by Billy Martin, got a ton of innings from their starters (Steve McCatty 221; Matt Keough 250; Mike Norris 284; Rick Langford 290). With the exception of Norris, who made a brief comeback in 1990 after a six-year hiatus, all four pitchers were out of the majors by 1987.

8. Duke Snider and Mickey Mantle (*4 points*)

The Duke led the National League in homers (43), on-base percentage (.402), and slugging average (.598) that year. Mantle had the best season of his career—one of the best in history. He won the Triple Crown, winning the home run "race" by 20, with 52. He also led the AL in runs and slugging average.

9. C) Alvin Crowder (*5 points*)

Alvin Crowder won 167 games over his 11-season career with the Senators, St. Louis Browns, and Detroit Tigers.

10. Troy Glaus and Mo Vaughn (*4 points*)

Glaus out-homered Vaughn 47–36, but his 2000 salary was $275,000 compared to Vaughn's $11,166,667.

11. Jack Clark (*6 points*)

Clark tied a club record by drawing 136 walks in 1987—he also hit 35 homers and drove in 106 runs in just 131 games that year. Clark shared that record until Mark McGwire shattered it by walking 162 times in 1998.

12. Joe Cronin and Hal Breeden (*7 points*)

Joe Cronin did it for the Boston Red Sox on June 17, 1943, and Hal Breeden did it for Montreal on July 13, 1973.

13. 1-b, 2-c, 3-e, 4-a, 5-g, 6-d, 7-f (5 of 7: *5 points*; 6 of 7: *6 points*; 7 of 7: *8 points*)

Fisk vs. Darcy in Game 6, 1975; Henrich vs. Newcombe in Game 1, 1949; Carter vs. Williams in Game 6, 1993; Gibson vs. Eckersley in Game 1, 1988; Mazeroski vs. Terry in Game 7,

1960; Matthews vs. Grim in Game 4, 1957; and Rhodes vs. Lemon in Game 1, 1954.

14. Cal Hubbard   (*5 points*)

The hard-nosed tackle starred for Centenary and Geneva colleges, and later for the New York Giants and Green Bay Packers in the NFL. He was voted into Cooperstown for his distinguished service as an American League umpire.

15. John Flaherty   (*6 points*)

Tampa Bay's John Flaherty threw out 38.6 percent of runners attempting to steal in 1999.

16. D) Steve Busby   (*4 points*)

Royals rookie Steve Busby no-hit the Tigers on April 27, 1973. In the first month since the designated hitter came into effect, Busby did not come to bat in the game. Nolan Ryan pitched the first of his seven no-hitters a few weeks later for the Angels.

17. C) Harry Lunte   (*5 points*)

Aside from being a baseball trivia answer, shortstop Harry Lunte batted .196 over his two-year major league career, winning a world championship with Cleveland in 1920.

18. Minnesota Twins   (*5 points*)

The Twins won Game 1 of the 1987 Series at the Metrodome, 10–1. They won their other three games played at the Metrodome against the Cardinals while losing all three in St. Louis. Minnesota won the World Series again in 1991 by winning all four games against the Braves in Minneapolis and losing all three in Atlanta.

19. Johnny Kling (*7 points*)

The Cubs catcher won the world pocket billiards title in 1909, and ran a successful pool hall in Kansas City, Missouri, after his baseball career.

20. A) Todd Worrell (*3 points*)

Worrell set the major league rookie record in 1986 for the St. Louis Cardinals. Gregg Olson set the AL rookie record with 27 saves for the 1989 Baltimore Orioles, but fell shy of the big league mark.

Top 2nd

1. Mike Schmidt, Willie Stargell, and Duke Snider
(2 of 3: *5 points*; 3 of 3: *7 points*)

All three have more than 400 career homers, and all three have plaques in Cooperstown.

2. Martin Dihigo (*5 points*)

Dihigo, arguably the greatest Cuban player of all time, is a Hall of Famer in the United States, Cuba, and Mexico. In his years in the Negro Leagues, he won three home run crowns and tied Josh Gibson for another. As a pitcher he racked up more than 200 wins in American and Mexican ball.

3. C) Denny Neagle (*3 points*)

Neagle made $4,750,000 in 1999 and started 19 games for the Reds; Wohlers appeared in two games, posted a 27.00 ERA, and made $5,200,000.

4. Cleveland Indians, Kansas City Athletics, New York Yankees, and St. Louis Cardinals (*3 points*)

Maris played for the Indians, Athletics, Yankees, and Cardinals, in that order. With the exception of his seven years in New York, his stays were all two-year stints.

5. Tris Speaker (*6 points*)

Cleveland's Tris Speaker hit .386 in 1916, beating out Cobb by 15 points. Speaker hit .345 over a 22-season career, but 1916 was his lone batting crown.

6. Bert Campaneris and Cesar Tovar (*5 points*)

Campaneris did it for the Kansas City Athletics in 1965, and Tovar did it for the Twins in 1968. Tovar was the only one of the four to start the game on the mound, pitching a hitless first inning and striking out a batter.

7. A) Johnny Blanchard (*4 points*)

Roseboro won it in the National League in 1961 and '66, Edwards won the NL award in '63 and '64, and Bench won NL Gold Gloves from 1968–77.

8. Rollie Fingers (*6 points*)

Reliever Rollie Fingers had only six winning seasons in the 17 he played, finishing with a career mark of 114–118.

9. Babe Ruth, Mel Ott, Jimmie Foxx, Johnny Mize, Wally Post, Willie Mays, Sammy Sosa, Norm Cash, Jim Rice, George Bell (7 of 10: *6 points*; 8 of 10: *8 points*; 10 of 10: *10 points*)

Some current players could also crack this list: Jose Cruz Jr., Jermaine Dye, Moises Alou, and Jeff Kent.

10. Dallas Green (*5 points*)

Green was a reliever with the Phillies in the early 1960s, and he led the 1980 Phils to a world championship with the help of Mike Schmidt's bat and Steve Carlton's arm.

11. C) Derek Bell (*3 points*)

Derek Bell pitched for Belmont Heights (Tampa), a team that also featured Gary Sheffield, in the 1981 Little League World Series. In his next pitching appearance, with the Mets in August 2000, Bell was lit up by the Padres for five runs in the eighth inning of a 16–1 loss. Colorado catcher Brent Mayne also made his major league mound debut that day, but he actually picked up a win with a scoreless inning against Atlanta.

12. Gaylord Perry and Jim Perry (*4 points*)

Gaylord and Jim Perry faced off in the 1974 All-Star Game in Cincinnati. Gaylord, a member of the Giants, pitched the sixth and seventh innings for the National League, while Jim of the Twins pitched the seventh and eighth for the AL. Neither figured in the decision, but the NL won the game in the 12th inning when hometown hero Pete Rose bowled over catcher Ray Fosse.

13. Otis Nixon (*4 points*)

Nixon stole 478 bases in the decade, beating out Rickey Henderson (463) and Kenny Lofton (433).

14. Warren Spahn (*6 points*)

Warren Spahn surrendered the first home run by Willie Mays,

ending an 0-for-21 slump to start his career. "I'll never forgive myself," Spahn said years later. "We might have gotten rid of Willie forever if I'd only struck him out."

15. D) Steve Carlton, 1980   (*4 points*)

"Lefty" Carlton not only pitched 304 innings, he also led the National League with 24 wins and 286 strikeouts. Carlton became the fourth pitcher to win three Cy Young Awards; two years later he became the first to win the award four times.

16. Wade Boggs   (*5 points*)

Wade Boggs had 240 hits for Boston in 1985, winning his first of four consecutive AL batting titles with a .368 average.

17. A) Dizzy Dean   (*5 points*)

Dean accomplished the feat in Game 7 of the 1934 World Series. Dizzy and his brother Paul won two games apiece in the Series, carrying the Cardinals past Detroit. Another freak occurrence in Game 7: Detroit fans threw food and bottles at Joe Medwick after his rough slide into third, prompting Commissioner Landis to order Medwick out of the game "for his own safety."

18. Mark Belanger, Ozzie Smith, and Omar Vizquel (*6 points*)

The Wizard swept the 1980s as the National League's best defensive shortstop, winning a record 13 consecutive Gold Gloves between 1980 and 1992.

19. Bucky Walters (*6 points*)

Bucky Walters of Cincinnati won a Triple Crown in 1939, leading the Reds to a pennant. He nearly made it back-to-back Triple Crowns the next season, leading the league in wins and ERA but falling short in strikeouts by 22.

20. C) Napoleon Lajoie (*3 points*)

Nap batted .426 in the American League's first year as a major league in 1901, winning the batting title by 86 points over Mike Donlin. It was the highest batting average of the century and, along with his 14 home runs and 125 RBIs, enabled Lajoie to win the Triple Crown. It was Lajoie's only season with the Athletics because of a lawsuit filed by his former NL employer, the Phillies. He sat out two months before Connie Mack sent him to Cleveland's AL entry, which was renamed the Naps the following season.

Bottom 2nd

1. A) Colorado Rockies (*4 points*)

The Rockies started Arizona's franchise history with a loss, but they would finish the season 77–85, only 12 games in front of the expansion D-backs.

2. Satchel Paige (*5 points*)

Satchel Paige debuted with the Cleveland Indians two days after his 42nd birthday.

3. Babe Ruth (*6 points*)

The names represent the succession of starting right fielders for the New York Yankees from 1919 to 1934. (Note: One occasionally encounters a "trick" trivia question that asks, "Which Hall of Famer did Babe Ruth replace in right field for the Yankees?" The "answer" is George Halas, a member of the Pro Football Hall of Fame. But although Halas was on the 1919 Yankees' roster, Vick was the team's regular right fielder.)

4. John Tudor (*5 points*)

John Tudor went 2–1 for the Cardinals in their 1985 Series loss to Kansas City. He made it back to the Series in 1987, but had a 1–1 record and a 5.73 ERA in another seven-game heartbreaker, this time at the hands of the Minnesota Twins.

5. Ralph Kiner (*3 points*)

In just 10 seasons in the majors, Kiner hit 369 home runs, had 1,015 RBIs, and drew 1,011 walks.

6. C) Jim Mason (*5 points*)

Jim Mason of the Yankees hit a solo homer in Game 3 of the 1976 World Series.

7. Vince Coleman (*3 points*)

In 1987 Vince Coleman stole 109 bases to lead the major leagues. It was the third and last 100-steal season of his career, and the last time anyone reached three-digit territory. All-time stolen base king Rickey Henderson, who set a modern record with 132 steals in 1982, stole 100 bases for the third and last time in 1983.

8. Texas Rangers (*6 points*)

Hall of Fame umpire Nestor Chylak declared that the game should be forfeited to the Rangers. Following an Indians rally to tie the game in the ninth, fans swarmed onto the field and attacked Rangers right fielder Jeff Burroughs and other players. A crowd of 25,134 downed an estimated 60,000 cups of beer at Municipal Stadium. Alcohol-related promotions were subsequently prohibited at major league parks.

9. Mel Ott and Paul O'Neill (*5 points*)

Ott hit 511 career homers, while O'Neill had 260 homers after the 2000 season.

10. Cristian Guzman (*4 points*)

In 2000 Minnesota's Cristian Guzman became the first American Leaguer in 15 years to hit 20 triples in a season. Willie Wilson hit 21 triples for the world champion Royals in 1985.

11. A) Joe Jackson   (*4 points*)

Shoeless Joe batted .408 in 1911, finishing second in the AL to Ty Cobb's .420. Jackson would finish second to Cobb in the batting race in 1912 and '13, as well.

12. Dave Kingman   (*5 points*)

Kingman started the 1977 season with the Mets, was traded to San Diego, then to California, and then, finally, to the Yankees. He ended up hitting 26 homers on the year, never batting higher than .250 for any of the four clubs.

13. C) Tommy John   (*5 points*)

Tommy John pitched in 26 seasons and lasted in the majors until he was 46, while Young played 21 seasons and retired at 44. John, however, pitched in "just" 760 games, while Young threw 749 complete games alone. Orosco, Eckersley, and Wilhelm each appeared in more than 1,000 games (the majority of those in relief).

14. Duke Snider 1957; Mickey Mantle 1958, 1960; Henry Aaron 1969, 1973; Harmon Killebrew 1963; Rico Petrocelli 1969; Davey Johnson 1973; Darryl Evans 1985 (5 of 7: *5 points*; 6 of 7: *6 points*; 7 of 7: *9 points*)

No player has done this in a while, but Anaheim's Troy Glaus came close in 2000, hitting 47 home runs with just 102 RBIs.

15. Clark Griffith   (*7 points*)

Clark Griffith won 21 games in 1894, with a 4.92 ERA. The highest ERA for a 20-game winner in the 20th century is 4.63, posted by Vern Kennedy of the White Sox in 1936.

16. Lou Boudreau (*5 points*)

Lou Boudreau led the 1948 Cleveland Indians to a world championship on the field and in the dugout. In addition to managing the team the entire season, Boudreau hit .355 with a .453 on-base, scored 116 runs, drove in 106, and led the AL in fielding average at shortstop. It almost goes without saying that he ran away with the AL MVP that year.

17. D) Ty Cobb (*5 points*)

Ty Cobb's 248 hits in 1911 had broken Jesse Burkett's standard of 240 in 1896. Willie Keeler had 239 hits in 1897, the year he hit in 44 straight games. Nap Lajoie had 232 hits in 1901 for the Philadelphia Athletics, establishing the AL record that Cobb would break a decade later.

18. 1915 Philadelphia Athletics (*5 points*)

The 1915 Philadelphia Athletics finished 43–109 (.283) after posting a mark of 99–53 (.651) the season before. After winning four pennants in five years, owner Connie Mack sold most of his starting players to other teams.

19. 1903 New York Giants (*5 points*)

The 1903 Giants, led by McGraw, McGinnity, and Mathewson, finished 84–55 (.604) after finishing 48–88 (.353) the year before.

20. B) Bobby Shantz (*4 points*)

Bobby Shantz, who won 18 games with the Philadelphia Athletics in 1951, lost to the Japanese, 3–1. The loss in Japan didn't affect Shantz in 1952, when he won a league-leading 24 games.

Top 3rd

1. Jeff Cirillo (*4 points*)

Colorado's Jeff Cirillo had 115 RBIs in 2000. He drove in more runs than Troy Glaus, who hit 47 home runs, and Tony Batista, who hit 41. There were 35 third basemen who hit more than Cirillo's 11 homers.

2. B) Nolan Ryan (*4 points*)

Nolan Ryan became the first player to earn $1 million in annual salary in 1980, when he signed a four-year contract with Houston. Mike Schmidt earned the first $500,000 salary in 1977.

3. Carlton Fisk (*5 points*)

Fisk went on to play six more years with the White Sox after he turned 40 in December 1987, hitting 72 homers in 537 games.

4. Nap Lajoie (*7 points*)

Lajoie hit 48 doubles for Cleveland in 1906 without hitting a home run. He actually led the American League in homers in 1901, when he turned in a monster season—by any era's standards. Nap won the Triple Crown and led the league in runs, hits, doubles, on-base percentage, slugging average, and fielding average at second base.

5. C) Gene Tenace (*4 points*)

Gene Tenace, who had just one hit in the 1972 ALCS for Oakland, homered twice off Cincinnati's Gary Nolan in Game

1 of the World Series. He hit two more homers in Oakland's seven-game win to earn Series MVP honors. In 1996 Andruw Jones of the Braves became the first NL player to homer in his first two World Series at bats.

6. Bobby Witt (*6 points*)

The Texas Rangers drafted Bobby Witt with the third overall pick. Witt walked 283 batters his first two seasons in the majors, but had a long career as a starter, amassing 138 wins over 14 seasons.

7. Detroit Tigers (*6 points*)

The Tigers had nine players make their debut that day because the entire team refused to play. They were incensed because of the suspension of Ty Cobb, who had leaped into the crowd to attack a heckler at New York's Hilltop Park three days earlier. The pickup team lost to the Philadelphia Athletics, 24–2; only one of the nine players making their debuts that day ever played again in the major leagues.

8. A) Kent Tekulve (*4 points*)

Kent Tekulve appeared in 399 games from 1976–80 while pitching out of the Pittsburgh bullpen. He pitched in 90 or more games three different seasons, and finished his career with 1,050 games, all in relief.

9. Dick Allen (*7 points*)

With 351 career homers, Allen is a very, very distant second to the No. 1 guy on this list. Allen played in six All-Star Games, twice led the AL in homers, and finished his career with a .534 slugging average.

10. Chris Sabo (*5 points*)

Sabo played a great third base and made the All-Star team his
rookie year, and won a world championship with the Reds in
1990.

11. B) George Crowe (*4 points*)

George Crowe's career year was 1957, when he hit 31 homers
and drove in 92 runs for the Reds.

12. Ivan DeJesus and Larry Bowa (*4 points*)

The Cubs sent DeJesus to the Phillies in exchange for
Bowa and Sandberg. No. 1 draft pick Shawon Dunston
would eventually push Bowa into retirement, forming a
Sandberg–Dunston keystone combo that lasted 10 seasons.

13. Reggie Jackson (*5 points*)

Reggie went into the Hall all by himself in 1993. Phil Niekro,
Orlando Cepeda, and Tony Perez fell short by less than 100
votes (all three would be voted in later).

14. Roy Campanella, Ted Kluszewski, Carl Yastrzemski, and
Rico Petrocelli (3 of 4: *5 points*; 4 of 4: *6 points*)

There are a ton of names that have come close to making this
list (Gary Sheffield being the latest nine-letter guy to hit 40
homers), but these are the only four that fit the description.

15. B) Ed Kranepool (*3 points*)

"Steady Eddie" Kranepool signed with the Mets out of James
Madison High School in the Bronx at age 17, and appeared

with the club in its inaugural season in 1962. He remained with the team through the bad, the good, and then the bad some more, until he finally hung up his spikes in 1979.

16. 1995 Kansas City Royals (*7 points*)

The 1995 Royals were 70–74 and finished 30 games behind the Cleveland Indians.

17. D) Gaylord Perry (*4 points*)

Gaylord Perry lasted 15 innings for the Cleveland Indians on April 17, 1974. He gave up four runs on eight hits and four walks, while striking out 14 Milwaukee Brewers. He did not figure in the decision.

18. Cincinnati Reds (*4 points*)

Lee Smith, John Franco, Randy Myers, and Jeff Reardon all played for the Reds during their careers.

19. Philadelphia Phillies (*8 points*)

From 1891–95, they started Ed Delahanty in left, Billy Hamilton in center, and Sam Thompson in right.

20. Carlos May (*3 points*)

Carlos May wore his date of birth on his back (May 17). He was born in Birmingham, Alabama, in 1948.

Bottom 3rd

1. B) Charlie Hough   (*4 points*)

Jackson's solo homer was the only earned run Hough allowed in the Series in five innings of work.

2. Todd Zeile   (*5 points*)

Former catcher Todd Zeile took over third base for the Cardinals in 1991, and would stay there until 1995. Pendleton moved on to Atlanta, where he would win a batting title, an MVP Award, and a National League pennant in his first year with the Braves.

3. C) Al Lopez   (*4 points*)

Al Lopez led the 1954 Indians and 1959 White Sox to pennants to break the Yankees' stranglehold on the AL. His clubs finished second to the Yanks eight times in 13 seasons, and placed second 10 times in all. He was elected to the Hall of Fame in 1977.

4. Ty Cobb and George Sisler   (*6 points*)

Paul Molitor just missed this group in 1987, when he strung together a 39-game streak; Molitor's was the longest streak in the American League since Joltin' Joe's.

5. Ron Guidry   (*5 points*)

Guidry went 25–3 for the Yankees in his banner year of 1978. He led the AL with nine shutouts and a 1.74 ERA. The highest single-season winning percentage for any pitcher is .947—Roy Face went 18–1 out of the bullpen for Pittsburgh in 1959.

6. A) Los Angeles Angels (*3 points*)

The Angels finished eighth in 1961, but their 70 wins remain the best mark by a first-year team. Although the Marlins and Diamondbacks both just barely missed 100 losses in their inaugural campaigns, Florida won a World Series in just its fifth season, while Arizona won a division title in its second year. The Angels were around 19 seasons before reaching the playoffs—as were the Mariners.

7. Jimmy Dykes (*6 points*)

In 22 seasons Jimmy Dykes managed 2,962 games without ever finishing higher than third place.

8. Manny Ramirez (*5 points*)

Cleveland's Manny Ramirez had a .457 on-base percentage and a .697 slugging average—comfortably ahead of Barry Bonds, the No. 2 outfielder in those categories.

9. "No eating crackers in bed" (*8 points*)

In the game's early years, players not only roomed together but often shared a bed while on the road. Schreckengost, fed up with the nocturnal habits of his battery mate, held out for a "no eating crackers in bed" clause in both their contracts. Connie Mack gave in, and Schreck's contract was renewed. The mandatory diet amendment might've been good for the Rube: He struck out 349 batters in 1904, a record that stood until Sandy Koufax broke it 61 years later.

10. D) Willie Mays (*5 points*)

Mays finished in the top 5 in MVP balloting nine times over his 22-season career. He won the NL MVP Award in 1954 and

1965, but his best season was probably 1955: He hit a league-high 51 homers, drove in 127 runs, and scored 123.

11. Frank Thomas and Frank Thomas (*6 points*)

After his bounceback 2000 season, the Big Hurt had 344 career homers. The other Frank Thomas—an outfielder who played in the '50s and '60s—hit 286 homers for seven different National League teams.

12. B) 1958 (*4 points*)

The defending world champion Milwaukee Braves won Game 4 of the 1958 World Series to take a three-games-to-one lead over the Yankees, but lost the next three games. The franchise was later swept by the Mets in the first NLCS in 1969, and was swept by St. Louis in the 1982 NLCS.

13. D) Jimmy Sheckard (*5 points*)

With Brooklyn, Sheckard batted .354 in 1901 and .332 in 1903, but never hit higher than .276 in any of his final eight seasons.

14. Robin Roberts (*4 points*)

Roberts Roberts is the only pitcher in history to allow 500 home runs. He also won 20-plus games six years in a row for the Phillies, from 1950–55.

15. Jeff Bagwell (*4 points*)

In Houston's miserable 2000 season, Jeff Bagwell became the first player since Ted Williams to score 150 or more runs in a season. Babe Ruth holds the modern record for runs in a season, with 177 in 1921.

16. Walter Johnson   (*5 points*)

Walter Johnson won the Chalmers Award—the earliest incarnation of the MVP Award—in 1913. The major leagues voted their MVPs from 1922–29, and the Baseball Writers' Association of America has awarded MVPs since 1931. Lefty Grove was the first pitcher to win the modern Award, beating out Lou Gehrig for the 1931 AL MVP.

17. Tommy Davis, Roberto Clemente, and Bill Madlock
(2 of 3: *5 points*; 3 of 3: *6 points*)

Tommy Davis won back-to-back batting titles for the Dodgers in 1962–63, Clemente then won the next two titles, and Madlock was batting champ for the Cubs in 1975–76. The last NL player to accomplish the feat was Colorado's Larry Walker, in 1998–99.

18. C) Honus Wagner   (*5 points*)

Honus Wagner held the title of baseball's hit king from 1916–23. Wagner had broken the mark set by Cap Anson. Tris Speaker later passed Wagner as well, but he retired a distant second to Cobb.

19. B) 34 percent   (*5 points*)

Thirty-four percent of the century's world champions led their league in homers. The correlation was more common in the first half of the century, when the New York Yankees typically led the AL in homers in years they won it all.

20. Joe Medwick (*5 points*)

In 1937 Joe Medwick of the Cardinals led the NL in home runs (31), RBIs (154), and batting average (.374).

Top 4th

1. a) Ken Williams; b) Wally Berger; c) Jimmie Foxx; d) Eddie Matthews; e) Duke Snider; f) Mel Ott; g) Roy Sievers; h) Norm Sieborn; i) Don Mincher; j) Frank Howard   (5 of 10: *6 points*; 8 of 10: *8 points*; 9 of 10: *9 points*; 10 of 10: *10 points*)

Williams hit 185 home runs from 1918–27; Berger hit 199, 1930–37; Foxx hit 302, 1925–35; Matthews hit 452, 1953–65; Snider hit 316, 1947–57; Ott hit 511, 1926–47; Sievers hit 180, 1954–59; Sieborn hit 75, 1960–63; Mincher hit 25, 1969; and Howard hit 237, 1965–71.

2. Charlie Robertson (*7 points*)

Charlie Robertson of the Chicago White Sox pitched a perfect game at Detroit on April 30, 1922, and finished his career with a 49–80 record.

3. Dave Kingman (*4 points*)

Kingman hit 48 homers for the Chicago Cubs in 1979, his career year. He also had the league's highest slugging average at .613 (Schmidt was a distant second at .564).

4. Nolan Ryan (30 and 34), Henry Aaron (44), Rod Carew (29), Frank Robinson (20), and Casey Stengel (37) (4 of 5: *4 points*; 5 of 5: *5 points*)

Ryan is the only player to have his uniform number retired by three franchises (Angels, Astros, Rangers), while Aaron, Carew, Robinson, and Stengel each had their numbers retired by two teams.

5. A) Jeff Kent (*3 points*)

Jeff Kent did not leave the yard once in 148 at bats against lefties in 1993 with the Mets. Through 2000 Kent had 194 career homers, only 32 of those coming off lefthanded pitching.

6. Willie Mays, Orlando Cepeda, and Willie McCovey (*5 points*)

These three Hall of Famers wasted no' time in making names for themselves in the majors. The Giants produced two ROYs in the 1970s—Gary Matthews in '73 and John Montefusco in '75—but haven't had one since.

7. Ted, Billy, Matt, and Cy (3 of 4: *3 points*; 4 of 4: *5 points*)

After the 2000 season, Matt Williams had 346 career homers, and will be hard-pressed to catch Billy's 426 before he retires. Cy Williams was an outfielder for the Cubs and Phillies from 1912–30. He was one of the great sluggers of the 1920s; playing in Philadelphia's Baker Bowl, he became the third player in major league history to hit 40 homers in a season in 1923.

8. D) NL West (*3 points*)

The NL West is one of only two divisions—the NL East is the other—that the Brewers haven't represented. They were an AL West club in 1970 and '71. When the Washington Senators moved to Texas in 1972, Milwaukee moved to the AL East.

When three divisions were added in 1994, the Brewers switched to the AL Central. In 1998 they became the first team to switch from the American to the National League, and took up residence in the NL Central.

9. Joe Nuxhall   (*5 points*)

Joe Nuxhall appeared in one game for the Cincinnati Reds on June 10, 1944, at the age of 15. After pitching two-thirds of an inning, he was sent to the minors and did not return until 1952.

10. Detroit Tigers   (*5 points*)

The 1961 Tigers were 101–61, but still weren't even close to the Mantle and Maris Yankees (109–53).

11. D) Frank Chance   (*4 points*)

Player-manager Frank Chance guided the Cubs to an astonishing .763 winning percentage   (116-36) in his first full season as skipper in 1906. The first baseman had taken over the team for ill Frank Selee and had won 55 of 90 games. In eight seasons with the club, Chance's Cubs had a .664 winning percentage, won four pennants, and captured two world championships.

12. Gil Hodges   (*5 points*)

Hodges finished his career with 370 homers, 12 behind Frank Howard.

13. B) Pete Rose   (*5 points*)

Pete Rose led the National League with a .394 mark in 1968, the year of the pitcher. The league OBP that year was just .302, but the Reds had by far and away the league's most potent offense. The young cogs of the Big Red Machine led the league in batting by 21 points, on-base by 12 points, and slugging by 23 points.

14. Jack Quinn (*5 points*)

Jack Quinn started Game 4 of the 1929 Series for the Philadelphia Athletics. He didn't get a decision, but Quinn's Athletics won the game and went on to win the Series.

15. Ken Brett (*5 points*)

Ken Brett was 19 when he made two scoreless relief appearances for the Boston Red Sox in the 1967 World Series.

16. C) Catfish Hunter (*4 points*)

Hunter defeated Dave McNally and the Orioles in Game 2 of the 1973 ALCS, 6–3. It was the first time Baltimore had lost an ALCS game, after sweeps of Minnesota in 1969 and 1970, and Oakland in 1971. Ken Holtzman defeated the O's the next day, and Hunter tossed a shutout to clinch the best-of-five series.

17. Kevin McReynolds (*5 points*)

Never really known for his basestealing until setting this record, Kevin McReynolds stole 21 bases without being caught in 1988 with the Mets. A quiet, steady left fielder with a great glove, McReynolds hit .265 over 12 seasons.

18. Hoyt Wilhelm (*6 points*)

One of the all-time great relief pitchers, Wilhelm compiled 143 wins and a 2.52 ERA over 21 seasons. He led the league in ERA and went 15–3 out of the pen for the Giants in his rookie season of 1952, and when Baltimore called on him to start 27 games in 1959, he led the league in ERA and made the All-Star team.

19. A) Chuck Klein   (*4 points*)

Chuck Klein had 107 extra-base hits in 1930 and 103 in 1932. Despite these Ruthian achievements—incidentally, in 1921 the Babe was the first player to reach the three-digit mark in extra-base hits—Klein's Phillies finished last in 1930 and fourth in '32.

20. John Tudor   (*5 points*)

John Tudor anchored the St. Louis pitching rotation in 1985, leading the Cards to a pennant. Tudor went 21–8 with a 1.93 ERA, finishing second to Dwight Gooden in the Cy Young Award vote.

Bottom 4th

1. Albert Belle   (*4 points*)

Albert Belle hit 52 doubles and 50 homers while leading the Cleveland Indians to the AL pennant in 1995. Belle led or tied for the league lead in doubles, homers, runs, RBIs, and slugging, and missed winning the AL MVP by eight votes.

2. D) None of the above   (*4 points*)

The next time a team scores 20 runs in a World Series game will be the first time. In 116 years, no team has ever accomplished the feat.

3. Gene Mauch   (*5 points*)

Gene Mauch had 1,902 wins in 27 seasons with the Phillies, Expos, Twins, and Angels.

4. B) Fred Lynn   (*3 points*)

Boston's Fred Lynn won both the Rookie of the Year and MVP Awards in the American League in 1975. Frank Robinson was named National League Rookie of the Year in 1956 and went on to win MVP Awards in both leagues. Rod Carew was AL Rookie of the Year in 1967, but didn't win an MVP until 10 years later. Thurman Munson was the AL's top rookie in 1970 and MVP in 1976.

5. D) Jim Barr   (*5 points*)

San Francisco's Jim Barr retired 41 hitters in a row in 1972, setting down the final 21 he faced on August 23 and the first 20 he faced on August 29.

6. A) Bobby Richardson   (*5 points*)

Bobby Richardson drove in 12 runs for the Yankees in the 1960 World Series.

7. Ty Cobb, Babe Ruth, Honus Wagner, Christy Mathewson, and Walter Johnson   (4 of 5: *5 points*; 5 of 5: *6 points*)

If the Hall of Fame loves good guys, its first balloting didn't show it—the above answer is given in the order of most votes received. Cobb garnered 222 votes, while Ruth and Wagner each got 215. Nap Lajoie, Tris Speaker, and Cy Young were inducted in 1937.

8. Doug Jones (*5 points*)

Doug Jones had 36 saves for the Milwaukee Brewers in 1997; he turned 40 in June of that year.

9. B) Lou Boudreau (*4 points*)

Between 1942–50 player-manager Lou Boudreau set the Indians mark for most managerial wins with 728, including a world championship in 1948. Player-manager Tris Speaker won Cleveland's only other 20th century world championship, in 1920. Al Lopez established the highest winning percentage by any Tribe manager (.617), but his 570 wins ranked fourth on the club's list.

10. Mitch Williams (*3 points*)

Williams delivered the pitch that ended it all. Carter drove the "Wild Thing's" offering over the left field fence with one out in the bottom of the ninth in Game 6 to give Toronto an 8–6 win. It was the second straight world championship for Toronto. Williams, who also blew a save in Game 4, had lost two leads for Curt Schilling in the NLCS.

11. 1978 Baltimore Orioles (*6 points*)

The 1978 Orioles posted a record of 90–72, finishing behind the Yankees, Red Sox, and Brewers in the American League East.

12. Nolan Ryan and Steve Carlton, respectively (*5 points*)

Aside from these two negative statistics, at least one of these two pitchers ranks in the top 10 in career wins, starts, shutouts, innings, hits per game, strikeouts, strikeouts per game, and opponents' batting average.

13. Vince Coleman *(5 points)*

Vince Coleman stole 472 bases for the Cardinals from his rookie year in 1985 to 1989. Stolen base king Rickey Henderson had one less steal during his best five-year stretch.

14. B) Cal Hubbard *(4 points)*

Former Green Bay tackle Cal Hubbard was an American League umpire from 1936–51, but he never played in a major league game. George Halas and Ernie Nevers had limited success as major leaguers, but both were inducted into the Pro Football Hall of Fame. Brian Jordan was an All-Pro in the NFL and an All-Star in the majors.

15. A) 17 *(3 points)*

The Rockies, playing at cavernous Mile High Stadium, reached the 1 million mark in just 17 dates in 1993. That broke the major league record set by the Blue Jays just a year earlier.

16. Bob Hendley and Lou Johnson
(1 of 2: *6 points*; 2 of 2: *8 points*)

Hendley was the losing pitcher, and Lou Johnson got the one hit, a double. Johnson would produce another big hit in a Koufax shutout in October: He broke a scoreless tie in Game 7 of the World Series with a solo homer off Minnesota's Jim Kaat, helping LA clinch the Series.

17. Bill Madlock *(4 points)*

Madlock spent just three seasons in Chicago, but won back-to-back batting titles in 1975 and '76. He won two more batting crowns with Pittsburgh in 1981 and '83.

18. Calvin Coolidge Julius Caesar Tuskahoma McLish
(*8 points*)

Only a pitcher could be born with a name like that. McLish pitched in the majors with little success from 1944–51, then disappeared into the bush leagues for four full seasons. He latched on with Cleveland in 1956 and went on to win 84 games over his last nine seasons.

19. Johnny Mize, Willie Mays, Mickey Mantle, Eddie Mathews, Willie McCovey, Kevin Mitchell, Tino Martinez, Roger Maris, Mark McGwire   (5 of 9: *5 points*; 7 of 9: *7 points*; 8 of 9: *8 points*; 9 of 9: *10 points*)

Some close calls: Willard Marshall hit 36 in 1947; Don Mattingly hit 35 in 1985; Lee May hit 38 in 1969 and 39 in 1971; and Edgar Martinez hit 37 in 2000.

20. A) Kansas City Royals   (*3 points*)

The Royals came back from a 3–1 deficit to beat Toronto in the 1985 ALCS (the first best-of-seven LCS), and then came back from 3–1 to beat the Cardinals in the World Series that year. An infamous call by umpire Don Denkinger helped keep a Royals rally alive in Game 6 against the Cardinals, and Kansas City throttled St. Louis the following night in the finale of the "I-80" Series.

Top 5th

1. B) Chuck McElroy   (*3 points*)

Chuck McElroy made 603 relief appearances before getting the call by Baltimore manager Mike Hargrove, whose team was playing its second doubleheader in nine days. McElroy, who pitched five shutout innings for the win against the contending Oakland A's, broke Mike Stanton's one-year-old mark of 552 relief appearances before his first start.

2. Gene Brabender   (*6 points*)

Brabender led the Pilots with 13 wins and 14 losses in 1969. Bud Selig bought the Pilots for $10,800,000 in 1970, and they were the Milwaukee Brewers from that year forward. Brabender went 6–15 in the Brewers' first season and was out of the majors by 1971.

3. D) Manny Mota   (*4 points*)

Manny Mota holds the career record for pinch hits with 150. Mota played 20 seasons in the National League, getting 400 at bats only once, in 1970. He was a career .304 hitter for the Giants, Pirates, Expos, and Dodgers.

4. Shortstop   (*4 points*)

Derek Jeter will have stiff competition for the honor, battling Vizquel and Garciaparra throughout his career.

5. Duke Snider   (*6 points*)

Duke Snider hit 11 in six trips to the World Series with the Dodgers.

6. B) Cincinnati Reds   (*5 points*)

In a battle for third-place money, the Reds played three games in one day at Forbes Field. Cincy scored 20 runs in winning the first two games, but the tuckered-out Reds were shut out in the third game of the day. Cincinnati locked up third place.

7. Steve Carlton   (*5 points*)

Carlton won his fourth NL Cy Young Award in 1982, leading the league in wins, complete games, shutouts, innings, and strikeouts. Lefty hung on until 1988, but '82 was his last great season.

8. C) Cesar Geronimo   (*5 points*)

Reds center fielder Cesar Geronimo was Bob Gibson's 3,000th strikeout victim on July 17, 1974; on July 4, 1980, Nolan Ryan also fanned Geronimo to reach that milestone. The only others to be 3000th-strikeout victims during that span were Steve O'Neill of the Indians in 1923 (by Walter Johnson) and Joe Simpson of the Dodgers in 1978 (by Gaylord Perry).

9. Arizona Diamondbacks   (*6 points*)

Wagner turned in a huge season, striking out 111 of the 211 righthanded batters he faced—but the D-backs had his number. If not for a five-run pounding by Arizona early in the season, Wagner's 1999 ERA would have been 0.96.

10. Mel Ott   (*4 points*)

Mel Ott tops the franchise list with 1,860 career RBIs. Willie Mays finished his Giants career right behind him with 1,859.

11. C) Leo Durocher   (*5 points*)

Leo "The Lip" Durocher lined out to Cincinnati center fielder Harry Craft to end Vander Meer's second straight no-hitter on June 15, 1938. Vander Meer and catcher Ernie Lombardi thought they had struck out Durocher on the pitch before, but Bill Stewart called it a ball; the umpire later admitted he missed it in the dim light at the first night game at Ebbets Field.

12. Eleven (*6 points*)

Charles Pick of the Boston Braves wore an 0-for-11 collar in a 26-inning game against Brooklyn on May 1, 1920. The game—which ended in a 1–1 tie—is the longest in major league history.

13. A) Latroy Hawkins (*4 points*)

Latroy Hawkins of the Minnesota Twins lost his fourth game of the 1998 season in Wells' May 17 perfect game. Hawkins wasn't awful, allowing six hits and no walks in seven innings—but he needed to be perfect that day.

14. Rico Carty of the Atlanta Braves (*6 points*)

Rico Carty batted .366 to lead the National League in 1970. It was the highlight of Carty's outstanding but injury-filled career. He missed all of 1968 with tuberculosis, separated his shoulder seven times in 1969, and followed up his batting crown by breaking his kneecap and missing all of 1971.

15. Warren Spahn (*4 points*)

Warren Spahn was an All-Star selection 14 times, a record for pitchers. He pitched in seven Midsummer Classics without ever winning the game's MVP award.

16. A) Willie Aikens (*4 points*)

Aikens hit .400 with four homers and eight RBIs in a losing effort. Philadelphia took the Series in six games, with Mike Schmidt winning Series MVP honors.

17. Eddie Collins (*5 points*)

Collins scored 1,821 runs, and is seventh on the all-time stolen base list with 744. He batted .333 for his career without ever winning a batting title.

18. D) Gil Hodges (*5 points*)

Beloved Brooklyn first baseman Gil Hodges drove in the final run at Ebbets Field, as the Dodgers edged the Phillies on Danny McDevitt's 2–0 shutout on September 24, 1957. Five years later Hodges hit the first home run for the New York Mets.

19. B) Wes Ferrell (*5 points*)

Wes Ferrell hit nine home runs—the single-season record for pitchers—in 1931. He went 22–12 for Cleveland that year, with 30 RBIs and a whopping .621 slugging average. Ferrell hit .280 with 38 homers over his 15-year career.

20. Ted Williams and Mickey Cochrane (*8 points*)

The Splendid Splinter's was hit off Jack Fisher on September 28, 1960. Cochrane's homer came off the Yankees' Bump Hadley on May 25, 1937. On his next trip to the plate Cochrane took a pitch to the head, and the resultant skull fracture ended his career.

Bottom 5th

1. B) Dave Steib (*4 points*)

Dave Stieb, one of the best pitchers of Toronto's short franchise history, accomplished the feat on September 24 and 30,

1988. Stieb pitched in seven All-Star Games and holds club records for career starts, complete games, shutouts, wins, strikeouts, and ERA.

2. Jimmie Foxx, Stan Musial, Joe DiMaggio, Yogi Berra, Roy Campanella, Mickey Mantle, and Barry Bonds (4 of 7: *6 points*; 6 of 7: *7 points*; 7 of 7: *8 points*)

Musial had the most near-misses of the group, finishing second in the vote four times. If you change those second-places to first-places, Musial would have won seven MVPs in 15 years and four consecutively from 1948–51.

3. C) 1922 (*5 points*)

In 1922 the New York Giants swept the Yankees 4–0, but there was a tie in Game 2—the last Series game to end in a tie.

4. Danny Ainge (*3 points*)

Ainge played parts of three seasons with the Blue Jays, but decided to stick to basketball when he batted just .187 in 86 games in 1981. He was a key component of the Bird–McHale–Parish teams that dominated the 1980s.

5. Carlton Fisk (*5 points*)

Carlton Fisk stole three bases in three attempts in 1992 at the age of 44.

6. C) Tony Phillips (*4 points*)

Tony Phillips beat out Rickey Henderson by one walk (977–976) for third place in the decade. The top two are Barry Bonds with 1,146 walks and Frank Thomas with 1,076.

7. Mike Caldwell, Mike Flanagan, and Mike Willis
(2 of 3: *4 points*; 3 of 3: *6 points*)

Caldwell went 22–9 for Milwaukee in 1978, leading the league in complete games with 23. Flanagan won 19 for Baltimore and made the All-Star team. Mike Willis went 3–7 for Toronto, almost exclusively out of the bullpen, and finished his five-year career with a 7–21 record.

8. A) 12 (*5 points*)

Baker led the American League in home runs four straight years, from 1911–14, but never hit more than 12 in any of his 14 seasons. He was voted into the Hall of Fame by the Veterans Committee in 1955.

9. C) George Bradley (*5 points*)

Bradley was a pitcher, outfielder, and third baseman with eight teams in four different leagues from 1875–84. The first year of the National League was also Bradley's career year: He went 45–19 for St. Louis, leading the league in shutouts (16, a major league record) and ERA (1.23). His NL career fizzled after '76; he went 31–63 over the next two seasons.

10. New York Yankees, 1920; New York Yankees, 1946; Los Angeles Dodgers, 1978; Toronto Blue Jays, 1991 (3 of 4: *4 points*; 4 of 4: *6 points*)

The 1920 Yankees finished third, but Babe Ruth wowed fans by hitting 54 home runs—more than any other *team* in the AL. The 1946 Yankees also finished third, but many players came back from military service that year—including Joe DiMaggio. The 1978 Dodgers led the NL in homers and won the pennant. The 1991 Blue Jays, playing their third season in the SkyDome, won the AL East with an exciting young team.

11. First baseman Kent Hrbek, shortstop Greg Gagne, left fielder Dan Gladden, and center fielder Kirby Puckett (3 of 4: *4 points*; 4 of 4: *6 points*)

Tom Kelly led the worst-to-first '91 Twins to a championship with only these four holdovers from the '87 team and a completely revamped pitching staff that featured World Series MVP Jack Morris.

12. C) 1908 (*5 points*)

The next World Series home run was not hit until 1908. Five years and 23 Series games passed between Patsy Dougherty's second home run of Game 2 of the 1903 World Series and Joe Tinker's clout for the Cubs in Game 2 of the 1908 Series.

13. Ken Hunt (*6 points*)

Not to be confused with outfielder Ken Hunt, who played in the majors from 1959–64. Hunt went 9–10 for Cincinnati during the regular season, and pitched a scoreless ninth in the fifth and final game of the 1961 World Series, won by the Yankees.

14. Jimmie Foxx, Mickey Mantle, Brady Anderson, Sammy Sosa, Greg Vaughn, and Mark McGwire (4 of 6: *4 points*; 5 of 6: *5 points*; 6 of 6: *6 points*)

McGwire had 58 in 1997, but 34 were hit in the American League and 24 in the National League. Sosa, of course, twice hit more than 60, only to finish second both times to McGwire.

15. B) Burleigh Grimes (*5 points*)

Burleigh Grimes threw the last legal spitball in 1934. "Ol' Stubblebeard" used the spitball to earn 270 career wins with six teams from 1916–34. Gaylord Perry admitted to throwing the spitter, but he didn't do it legally.

16. B) Triple for his 3,000th hit (*4 points*)

Paul Molitor became the first player to hit a triple on his land-mark hit. Ironically, Molitor led the American League in singles in 1996. Dave Winfield did it in a Twins uniform in 1993. In 1999 Wade Boggs became the first player to homer for his 3,000th hit.

17. A) Lou Gehrig (*4 points*)

Lou Gehrig hit four homers, drove in nine runs, and drew six walks in the 1928 World Series. Gehrig and Ruth went a combined 16-for-27 with seven homers, as the Yankees dominated the Cardinals in a four-game sweep.

18. Gus Zernial and Richie Zisk (*4 points*)

Zernial leads the way with 237 career homers; Zisk hit 207, but Todd Zeile is right behind him, finishing the 2000 season at 205.

19. A) St. Louis Cardinals (*4 points*)

The Cardinals defeated the Brooklyn Dodgers in the best-of-three series to decide the 1946 pennant. It marked the first time that additional games were added at the end of the regular schedule to settle a first-place tie. St. Louis went on to defeat the Red Sox in the World Series.

20. Lee and Larry MacPhail (*5 points*)

In 1998 the MacPhails became the first father-son combo to enter the Hall of Fame, but neither got in for their playing ability. Lee and Larry MacPhail were baseball executives. Lee (enshrined in 1978) pushed for night baseball and radio broadcasts of home games, and he later became a part owner of the Yankees. Larry was quiet, but he accomplished plenty as director of player personnel with the Yankees and later as GM of the Orioles. He spent a decade as AL president.

Top 6th

1. Chicago White Sox   (*5 points*)

One of the greatest outfielders in baseball history played for the White Sox, but as of 2001 "Shoeless" Joe Jackson was still locked out of Cooperstown because of his involvement in the 1919 World Series scandal.

2. A) Jay Bell   (*4 points*)

Jay Bell earned his only Gold Glove Award at shortstop for the Pirates in 1993. Larkin and Ordonez would go on to win the award multiple times. Clayton, who succeeded Smith in St. Louis as the everyday shortstop in 1996, made 27 errors in his first season as a major league regular with the Giants in 1993.

3. 1918 Boston Red Sox and 1919 Cincinnati Reds
(*7 points*)

The Boston Red Sox and Cincinnati Reds won world championships in 1918 and 1919 without hitting a single homer. The 1918 Red Sox batted .186 in a six-game Series against the Chicago Cubs; the Cubs outscored the Sox 10–9, but batted just .210 themselves and lost every one-run game in the Series. The 1919 Reds defeated the Chicago "Black Sox" in eight games, outscoring the Sox 35–20 in the tainted Series.

4. A) Richie Hebner (*5 points*)

Richie Hebner played for the Pirates 1970–72 and 1974–75, and the Phillies in 1977 and 1978. He later appeared with the NL East champion Cubs in 1984. Bob Robertson was on five Eastern Division champions and Dave Cash was on four during the 1970s.

5. D) Rabbit Maranville (*4 points*)

Maranville, an excellent defensive shortstop, played 23 seasons with five different teams without ever leading the NL in anything other than fielding average.

6. Willie Wilson and Juan Samuel (*5 points*)

Willie Wilson had 705 at bats for the Royals in 1980, and Juan Samuel had 701 for Philadelphia in 1984. Eight different players have had 690 or more at bats in a season, most recently Colorado's Neifi Perez in 1999.

7. Greg Maddux (*6 points*)

Greg Maddux dominated the National League throughout the '90s, but never had more than 20 wins. He's won 20 games twice—his Cy Young seasons of '92 and '93—and 19 games five times, including three of the last five seasons.

8. C) Nellie Briles (*5 points*)

Nelson Briles was a 5–2 winner in Game 3 of the 1967 World Series, the only game Bob Gibson didn't win for St. Louis. Steve Carlton had a loss for the Cards in the Series and Hal Woodeshick had a no decision in one appearance. Roger Craig earned a win for St. Louis in the 1964 World Series.

9. 25th inning, Harold Baines (*6 points*)

Harold Baines of the Chicago White Sox homered in the 25th inning of a game against the Milwaukee Brewers on May 9, 1984.

10. B) Oakland and Chicago White Sox (*5 points*)

Johnson fanned 19 Oakland A's on June 24 (but lost) and struck out 19 White Sox on August 8 (and won). Despite these two great outings, he placed second in strikeouts for the year, finishing one whiff behind Roger Clemens (292–291).

11. B) Frank Schulte (*5 points*)

Frank Schulte of the Chicago Cubs hit 21 home runs in 1911, five more than Sam Crawford's previous 20th century record. The first 20th century player to hit 25 homers in a season was Babe Ruth, with 29 in 1919.

12. Billy Martin (*5 points*)

Martin took the 1970 Twins, 1972 Tigers, 1976–77 Yankees, and 1981 Athletics to the playoffs. The '77 Yankees were the only world championship team of the group.

13. Cincinnati Reds (*4 points*)

The great Reds teams have typically won on the strength of their bats and bullpens. Some of their Cy near-misses: Tom Seaver in 1981, Mario Soto in 1983, Danny Jackson in 1988, Pete Schourek in 1995.

14. Tim Raines (*4 points*)

Tim Raines stole 190 bases for the Montreal Expos, finishing second, third, and fourth each season. Although Coleman's arrival marked the end of Raines' reign as the league's stolen base king, Tim won his first and only batting title in 1986.

15. Lou Gehrig (*5 points*)

On July 4, 1939, Lou Gehrig told 61,808 fans he considered himself "the luckiest man on the face of the earth." The Yankees then retired his uniform No. 4.

16. A) Carlos Delgado (*5 points*)

Toronto's Carlos Delgado led AL first basemen in errors with 14. With his 44 homers, 39 doubles, and 134 RBIs, his defensive lapses couldn't have been all that vexing.

17. C) Heinie Manush (*5 points*)

Manush, a hard-hitting outfielder, made it into one World Series, which was one more than any of the other three. He didn't make the most of his opportunity, batting an anemic .111 for the 1933 Washington Senators in their five-game loss to the New York Giants.

18. Robin Yount, Paul Molitor, and Jim Gantner (*7 points*)

Their careers overlapped with the Milwaukee Brewers from 1978–92. Yount and Molitor are both in the 3,000-hit club; Yount is a Hall of Famer and Molitor—with more hits and a higher lifetime batting average—should make it in on his first ballot. Wisconsin native Jim Gantner played his entire 17-year career in Milwaukee.

19. D) Bret Saberhagen (*4 points*)

Bret Saberhagen won the AL Gold Glove in 1989, the year he won his second Cy Young Award. Mark Langston won the award both before and after Saberhagen, winning seven in all. Jim Kaat won the Gold Glove a record 14 times (in both leagues), and Bobby Shantz won seven overall, including the first award in 1957.

20. Mickey Mantle, Frank Robinson, and Carl Yastrzemski (*4 points*)

There was a lot of Triple Crown talk late into the 2000 season, focused mainly on Toronto first baseman Carlos Delgado. He ended up falling well short of the feat, finishing tied for fourth in the AL in homers, tied for fourth in RBIs, and fourth in batting average.

Bottom 6th

1. Willie McCovey, Fred McGriff, and Kevin McReynolds (2 of 3: *5 points*; 3 of 3: *7 points*)

McCovey—a Hall of Famer and a member of the 500 home run club—should have been easy. The "Crime Dog" just passed the 400-homer plateau, and hit 30 or more home runs seven straight years from 1988–94. McReynolds was the tough one, just making the list with 211 homers.

2. C) Reggie Jackson (*4 points*)

Reggie Jackson carved out his niche as "Mr. October" in the 1977 Series, hitting five homers—three of them on consecutive swings in Game 6—in a six-game defeat of the Dodgers. The Yankees again beat the Dodgers in six to win the '78 Series, with Reggie hitting two homers and driving in eight.

3. C) Babe Ruth (*4 points*)

Babe Ruth hit four homers (with only five RBIs) in the 1926 Series loss to the Cardinals, two homers in the 1927 Series sweep of Pittsburgh, and three homers in a sweep of the Cardinals in 1928. Ruth's slugging average over the three World Series: 1.020.

4. One (*5 points*)

Blyleven was a league leader in strikeouts only once. He fanned 206 batters with the Twins and Indians to lead the AL in 1986, one of eight 200-strikeout seasons in his 22-year career.

5. Eddie Mathews (*5 points*)

Twenty-one-year-old Eddie Mathews led the league with 47 homers—Kiner hit 35. Mathews finished second in MVP balloting in the Braves' first year in Milwaukee.

6. B) John Wathan (*4 points*)

John Wathan managed the Angels for an 89-game stint in 1992, but was not a part of the 1994 California carousel.

7. Willie Mays (*4 points*)

Willie Mays hung it up on the losing side after his Mets lost to Oakland in seven games, as Reggie Jackson earned Series MVP honors. By that time Mays was reduced to a part-time player. During the contest, the "Say Hey Kid" collected two hits in six at bats.

8. A) Boston Beaneaters (*5 points*)

Led by manager Frank Selee and his concept of "scientific

baseball," the Beaneaters won 102 games in 1892 and repeated the feat in 1898. Boston's 102 wins are a 19th century record.

9. New York Mets (*6 points*)

The Mets selected Clemens in the 12th round of the 1981 free-agent draft. The Boston Red Sox made him their first-round pick in 1983; he quickly became their ace, leading the Sox to a seven-game World Series defeat in 1986, at the hands of . . . the Mets.

10. Ernie Banks and Barry Bonds (*5 points*)

After his monster 2000 season, Bonds is sitting on 494 career homers and should eclipse Banks's 512 in 2001.

11. New York Mets (*5 points*)

The Mets won the pennant with just 82 regular-season victories in 1973. Led by reliever Tug McGraw and his "Ya Gotta Believe" rallying cry, they were in last place at the end of August and in first place a little more than a month later. The Reds won 99 games in 1973 but lost the NLCS to a team that won 17 fewer games during the regular season. New York lost to Oakland in a seven-game World Series.

12. D) Sandy Koufax (*5 points*)

Koufax was more than a little talented, but also a bit of a pessimist.

13. A) Rocky Colavito (*5 points*)

Rocco Domenico Colavito had a perfect season in the outfield for Cleveland in 1965. He wasn't too bad at the plate either, leading the league with 108 RBIs and 93 walks.

14. 1932 New York Yankees (*7 points*)

With Ruth, Gehrig, and Lazzeri, the 1932 Yankees scored 6.4 runs per game and went on to sweep the Cubs in the World Series. The 2000 Reds averaged 5.1 runs a game and finished a distant second to St. Louis in the NL Central.

15. Darryl Strawberry, 1988 (*5 points*)

Darryl Strawberry led the NL with 39 homers in 1988, leading the Mets to a division title. Between 1980 and 1995, only Strawberry, Fred McGriff, and Barry Bonds won NL home run titles from the left side of the plate.

16. D) Guy Hecker (*5 points*)

Hecker hit three out on August 15, 1886, in the second game of a twin bill. Playing for Louisville in the American Association, he also scored seven runs in the game, establishing a record that as of 2000 has yet to be surpassed.

17. Zero (*4 points*)

Robin Yount won MVP Awards at two different positions, but no one has ever won Gold Gloves at different positions.

18. D) Mickey Lolich (*5 points*)

Lolich threw three complete-game victories in the 1968 Series. Bob Gibson had shut down the Tigers in Games 1 and 4, but Lolich beat him and the Cards in Game 7, giving Detroit its first world championship since 1945.

19. B) George Frazier (*5 points*)

Frazier only pitched 3 ⅔ innings of the 1981 Series, but he was ineffective enough to lose three games for the Yankees.

Frazier came out of the pen three times and had a 17.18 ERA, handing Games 3, 4, and 6 to the Dodgers, who won the Series in six.

20. Oakland Athletics   (*5 points*)

The Oakland A's stole three bases simultaneously, but manager Billy Martin received as much credit as the baserunners for its execution. The strangest part is that Rickey Henderson, who had his first 100-steal season for Oakland in 1980, wasn't even involved in the play: Wayne Gross stole second, Mitchell Page took third, and Dwayne Murphy swiped home.

Top 7th

1. D) Johnnie LeMaster   (*4 points*)

Hard-luck Johnnie LeMaster had a long season. He played for the Giants (62–100), Indians (60–102), and Pirates (57–104) in 1985. His highest batting average in his three stops was .155 in 22 games for Pittsburgh.

2. A stolen base   (*5 points*)

Neither team stole a base, but the Browns didn't do much of anything offensively. They batted .183 for the Series and scored just 12 runs in the six-game loss to the Cardinals.

3. A) Rip Sewell   (*4 points*)

Rip Sewell was having resounding success in the NL with his "eephus" pitch, but Williams homered off him to the delight of Teddy's hometown fans at Fenway Park. Sewell wasn't the same after the homer by Williams and finished the season with an 8–12 record.

4. Paul O'Neill (*4 points*)

O'Neill hit .359 and made the All-Star team in his second season with the Yankees. O'Neill never hit .300 in his six full seasons in Cincinnati, but hit .300 or better his first six years in New York.

5. Sandy Koufax (*4 points*)

Sandy Koufax received all 20 votes from writers in 1963, 1965, and 1966. He won all three when only one Cy Young Award was given out for both leagues.

6. D) Mel Stottlemyre (*4 points*)

Mel Stottlemyre beat the Indians, 6–1, on seven hits on April 6, 1974. The Yankees spent two seasons at Shea Stadium while Yankee Stadium was being renovated. Stottlemyre spent a decade at Shea as pitching coach for the Mets and later returned to Yankee Stadium as a coach for the Yanks.

7. One (*6 points*)

In 1892 the Boston Beaneaters swept the Cleveland Spiders, 5–0 with a tie. Hugh Duffy led the Boston offense with 12 hits in 26 at bats, while Kid Nichols and Jack Stivetts combined to go 4–0 with a 0.96 ERA.

8. A) Bob Gibson (*5 points*)

Bob Gibson stole five bases in 1969 and had 11 in his career. San Diego rookie Adam Eaton led all pitchers with two stolen bases in 2000.

9. Christy Mathewson (*6 points*)

Matty may have had the toughest luck of any pitcher in World Series history. In four Series appearances with the Giants he had a 5–5 record, winning just one world championship, in 1905. His numbers for the 1905, 1911, 1912, and 1913 Series: 101 ⅔ innings, 76 hits, 10 walks, four shutouts, 1.06 ERA.

10. B) Al Kaline (*4 points*)

Kaline twice hit 29 homers in seasons abbreviated by injuries.

11. A) Montreal Expos (*4 points*)

Youngblood singled with his second team of the day, the Expos, on August 4, 1982. He received word during an after-noon game against the Cubs that he had been traded to Montreal. He joined the Expos in Philadelphia, where they were playing a night game, and arrived in time to pinch-hit a single off Steve Carlton.

12. B) Walter Johnson (*6 points*)

In the days before the designated hitter, Walter Johnson batted .433 at the age of 38 for the Washington Senators in 1925. The "Big Train" had 547 career hits, including 41 triples and 24 home runs.

13. B) 1927 New York Yankees (*5 points*)

The "Murderers' Row" team placed center fielder Earle Combs and right fielder Babe Ruth in the Hall of Fame, but not left fielder Bob Meusel. The other lineups: 1924 Tigers—Ty Cobb, Harry Heilmann, Heinie Manush; 1926 Pirates—Max Carey, Kiki Cuyler, Paul Waner; 1927 Senators—Goose Goslin, Sam Rice, Tris Speaker.

14. Carl Yastrzemski, Rudy York, and Robin Yount (2 of 3: *5 points*; 3 of 3: *7 points*)

Yaz tops the list with 452, York hit 277, and 1999 Hall of Fame inductee Yount hit 251. The three were selected for All-Star teams a combined 28 times.

15. Wilbur Wood   (*6 points*)

Workhorse Wilbur Wood threw 376 ⅔ in 1972. He had four consecutive 20-win seasons for the White Sox between 1971–74, topping 320 innings each year.

16. A) Colorado Rockies   (*4 points*)

The Rockies finished second in the NL West, but went to the Division Series as the Wild Card champion. Colorado, in just its third year of existence, lost to eventual world champion Atlanta in four games. The Dodgers won the NL West in 1995, and they were the second-ever NL Wild Card in 1996.

17. Sandy Koufax, Bob Gibson, and Reggie Jackson (2 of 3: *5 points*; 3 of 3: *7 points*)

Bob Gibson won the honor in 1964 and 1967; Reggie Jackson in 1973 and 1977; and Sandy Koufax won it in 1963 and 1965. The three Hall of Famers won 10 world championships between them.

18. C) Ferris Fain   (*5 points*)

First baseman Ferris Fain hit .290 over his nine-year career, but broke out for .344 and .327 batting averages with the Philadelphia Athletics in 1951 and '52. Fain hit just 48 home runs in 3,930 at bats, but had a .425 career on-base percentage.

19. D) Manny Sanguillen   (*5 points*)

Manny Sanguillen, Pittsburgh's regular catcher the previous four years and a close friend of Clemente's, started in right field on April 6, 1973. He had two hits as Pittsburgh rallied for a 7–5 win over the Cardinals. Richie Zisk took over right field later that season and Sanguillen returned behind the plate. Dave Parker became the regular right fielder two seasons later.

20. Bruce Sutter (*5 points*)

Bruce Sutter of the Chicago Cubs went 6–6 when he won the award in 1979, winning the first of his four consecutive NL saves titles.

Bottom 7th

1. B) Dave Foutz   (*3 points*)

Dead-ball-era pitcher Dave Foutz is just percentage points ahead of Ford—.69014 to Ford's .69006. Foutz won 147 games from 1884–94 and twice drove in more than 100 runs in a season, playing regularly as an outfielder and first baseman. He played in five World Series: with the St. Louis Browns 1885–87 and the Brooklyn Bridegrooms in 1889 and 1890.

2. Nomar Garciaparra (*5 points*)

Alex Rodriguez's late-season slump allowed Nomar to edge him in OPS, 1.033–1.026.

3. D) Casey Stengel (*5 points*)

Casey Stengel hit an inside-the-park home run to break a ninth-inning tie, giving the Giants a win in Game 1 of the 1923 World Series—the first Series game ever played at Yankee Stadium. Stengel, who later managed the Yankees to

10 pennants, led the Giants with two homers in the Series; only Babe Ruth hit more.

4. Tim McCarver (*7 points*)

The Cardinals stole just three bases in the 1964 Series (none by Lou Brock), but one of them was a steal of home by McCarver. Although Bob Gibson stole the show by going 2–1 with 31 strikeouts, McCarver was the Series' leading hitter at .478, and he won Game 5 with a three-run homer in the 10th inning. The Cards defeated the Yankees in seven games.

5. 1940s (*4 points*)

The Phillies, Athletics, and Pirates failed to reach the World Series from 1932–49. The state of Pennsylvania went through a 28-year drought, 1931–59, without any of its teams winning a world championship.

6. A) Rawly Eastwick (*4 points*)

Rawly Eastwick led the talented Reds bullpen with 22 saves in 1975. He also led the league in saves the following year as the Reds won their second straight world title, but he saved just 18 more games over the final five years of his career.

7. Ray Schalk (*6 points*)

The Hall of Fame catcher had 30 steals in 1916.

8. C) Eight (*5 points*)

The Yankees swept the World Series in 1927, 1928, 1932, 1938, 1939, 1950, 1998, and 1999. How many times have the

Yankees been swept in a Series? Three: in 1922 by the Giants (with one tie), 1963 by the Dodgers, and 1976 by the Reds.

9. A) Don Sutton   (*5 points*)

Aside from Satchel Paige, who spent most of his career in the Negro Leagues, Sutton is the only non-reliever in the Hall of Fame with just one 20-win season to his credit.

10. Maury Wills   (*4 points*)

1960 was the first of six consecutive seasons in which Wills would lead the NL in steals. He became the first modern player to steal 100 bases in a season in 1962, and stole 586 bases over his career.

11. B) Rick Wise   (*5 points*)

Rick Wise retired 32 straight Cubs between the second and 12th innings. Wise, who finished with a five-hitter, singled in the bottom of the 12th to help the Phillies win, 4–3. After the season, Wise was traded to St. Louis for Steve Carlton.

12. B) Tommy Davis   (*6 points*)

Tommy Davis had a remarkable 1962 season with the Dodgers, leading the league with 230 hits, a .356 average, and 153 RBIs; but his 27 home runs were 22 short of league leader Willie Mays' total.

13. Marty Barrett   (*6 points*)

Marty Barrett went 13-for-30 for the Red Sox over the seven-game Series, along with five walks. But it wasn't quite enough, as the Series' leading hitter struck out against Jesse Orosco to end Game 7.

14. Jim Kaat (*3 points*)

Pitcher Jim Kaat won 16 Gold Glove Awards during his career—matched only by Hall of Fame third baseman Brooks Robinson.

15. 14 (*7 points*)

Henry Mathewson took the hill against Boston on October 5, 1906, and set a modern NL record by walking 14 batters in a 7–1 loss—his only major league decision.

16. B) Phil Niekro (*5 points*)

Phil Niekro led the NL in both wins (21) and losses (20) in 1979 for an Atlanta team that lost 94 games. Steve Carlton and Jerry Koosman both lost 20 games the year after winning 20 games during the 1970s, but both preceded Niekro. Although Anthony Young set a record with 27 consecutive losses in the 1990s, he did it over a two-year span.

17. C) Bob Feller (*5 points*)

Hall of Famer Bob Feller walked 208 while striking out 240 in his first big season, 1938. The Cleveland fireballer would walk more than 100 batters in a season seven more times in his career, but would also lead the league in wins and strikeouts six times each.

18. Babe Ruth, Jimmie Foxx, and Mark McGwire
(2 of 3: *3 points*; 3 of 3: *5 points*)

Ruth hit 467 in the 1920s, Foxx hit 415 in the 1930s, and McGwire hit 405 in the 1990s. In case you were wondering . . .

Hank Aaron hit 375 homers in the '60s, and Ken Griffey Jr. hit 382 in the '90s.

19. B) Richie Zisk (*5 points*)

Richie Zisk homered several times at Montreal's Jarry Park as a member of the Pirates, but he made history with a home run for the White Sox at the opening of baseball in Toronto on April 7, 1977.

20. Carlton Fisk (*5 points*)

New Hall of Famer Carlton Fisk finished his career with 376 home runs. Jimmie Foxx is No. 1 on this list, with 534 career homers.

Top 8th

1. Six (*3 points*)

"Dem Bums" used six different starters in 1955: Don Newcombe, Billy Loes, Roger Craig, Carl Erskine, Karl Spooner, and Johnny Podres, who started twice. The Dodgers had also used six starters in the 1947 World Series, but to no avail.

2. C) Boston Red Sox (*4 points*)

Tom Seaver toed the rubber for the last time with the Red Sox in 1986, but he didn't pitch against his former club, the Mets, during the 1986 World Series because of an injury. Seaver, who came to Boston from the Chicago White Sox in a deal for Steve Lyons on June 29, 1986, did not pitch again after the season.

3. Ken Williams   (*6 points*)

Ken Williams hit 39 homers and drove in 155 runs for the St. Louis Browns in 1922. Williams was a big-time slugger for the era, hitting 20-plus homers four times and finishing his career with a .530 slugging average.

4. C) .215   (*5 points*)

Mario Mendoza batted .215 for his nine-year career. It might have been even higher if not for an especially ugly .118 average in his final season with Texas in 1982. (The .188 average belonged to Minnie Mendoza, a light-hitting infielder not related to Mario, who played for the Twins in 1970.)

5. C) Robin Yount   (*5 points*)

Robin Yount of the Brewers had four hits in Game 1 and Game 5 of the 1982 World Series. Teammate Paul Molitor became the first player to have five hits in a World Series game, but didn't get four hits in a game again during that Series.

6. Tony Armas   (*5 points*)

Armas led the majors with 43 homers and 123 RBIs in 1984.

7. Greg Maddux (2.58), Jose Rijo (2.74), and Pedro Martinez (2.83)   (2 of 3: *5 points*; 3 of 3: *7 points*)

With the exception of Rijo, the top five in ERA in the '90s

should all find their way to Cooperstown—fourth and fifth on this list are Roger Clemens and Randy Johnson.

8. C) Mel Ott (*5 points*)

In 1929, his finest all-around offensive season, the New York Giants outfielder also took part in 12 double plays.

9. Ken Griffey Sr. and Ken Griffey Jr. (*4 points*)

Ken Sr. did it in 1980 for the National League, and Junior did it for the American League in 1992.

10. D) Walter Johnson (*5 points*)

Walter Johnson won the most career 1–0 games, 38 in all. As a member of the sometimes-punchless Washington Senators, the "Big Train" also lost the most 1–0 games (26). Grover Cleveland Alexander earned the most 1–0 wins in National League history, but his 17 wins "the hard way" are less than half Johnson's total.

11. D) Clint Hartung and Whitey Lockman (*5 points*)

Hartung was a big pitching and power-hitting prospect who never panned out. With the Giants rallying in the ninth, Don Mueller broke his ankle on a hard slide into third, and Hartung pinch ran for him. Whitey Lockman played outfield and first base for the Giants from 1945–57, finishing his career with a .279 batting average.

12. Gaylord Perry (*6 points*)

Perry went 24–16 for Cleveland in his Cy Young season of 1972. He's 15th on the all-time wins list with 314, but he's also sixth on the career losses list, with 265.

13. Ron LeFlore (*4 points*)

Ron LeFlore was first scouted by Detroit while he was serving time in a maximum security prison for armed robbery. He went on to be the starting center fielder for his hometown Tigers and led each league in stolen bases during his nine-year career. His story was later the subject of both a book and a movie.

14. Jim Palmer (*6 points*)

Palmer threw a four-hit shutout against Sandy Koufax in Game 2 of the 1966 Series—at 20 years, 11 months, and 21 days old. The Orioles embarrassed Los Angeles in the four-game sweep, throwing three complete-game shutouts in all (Wally Bunker in Game 3 and Dave McNally in Game 4).

15. Brooklyn Dodgers, New York Giants, Chicago Cubs, and Houston Astros (*5 points*)

Durocher managed the Brooklyn Dodgers from 1939–48, the New York Giants from 1948–55, the Chicago Cubs from 1966–72, and the Houston Astros from 1972–73.

16. C) Bernard Gilkey (*4 points*)

Bernard Gilkey homered off David Wells on June 17, 1998. It was the second regular-season game ever played between the two teams.

17. C) New York Mets (*4 points*)

The New York Mets paid $1.8 million to enter the NL in 1962. The Houston Colt .45s (later the Astros) paid just a bit more at $1.85 million that year. By contrast, the expansion Washington Senators and Anaheim Angels had paid $2.1 million each to the AL a year earlier.

18. Joe Tinker, Johnny Evers, Luis Aparicio, Edd Roush, Roger Bresnahan, Rick Ferrell, Ernie Lombardi, Ray Schalk   (3 of 8: *3 points*; 5 of 8: *5 points*; 7 of 8: *7 points*; 8 of 8: *9 points*)

These Hall of Famers were mostly renowned for their defense: With the exception of Roush, an outfielder, the rest of the players are middle infielders and catchers.

19. C) Bill McKechnie   (*4 points*)

McKechnie took the 1925 Pirates, 1928 Cardinals, and 1939–40 Reds to the Series. He played in the majors from 1907–20, and made his first managerial appearance as a playing manager with Newark of the Federal League in 1915. McKechnie went on to manage four NL teams over 24 seasons, winning 1,896 games.

20. Dave Righetti   (*4 points*)

Dave Righetti tossed a no-hitter on July 4, 1983, but that was his last year as a starter. In 1986 he set a major league record (since broken) with 46 saves. He saved 252 games and had only one other shutout besides his no-hitter.

Bottom 8th

1. Greg Vaughn and Mo Vaughn   (*6 points*)

After the 2000 season, Greg led Mo in the "V" home run race, 320–299.

2. D) Everett Scott   (*5 points*)

Slick-fielding shortstop Everett Scott completed a 1,307-game streak in 1925, the same year Gehrig—his rookie teammate—began his string.

3. 1979 Rick Sutcliffe, 1980 Steve Howe, 1981 Fernando Valenzuela, 1982 Steve Sax
(3 of 4: *3 points*; 4 of 4: *5 points*)

The Dodgers bettered that streak in the 1990s, producing five straight NL ROYs from 1992–96 (Eric Karros, Mike Piazza, Raul Mondesi, Hideo Nomo, and Todd Hollandsworth). First baseman Karros is the only one of the group still in Los Angeles.

4. D) Christy Mathewson   (*4 points*)

Christy Mathewson put together the most dominant pitching performance in World Series history in 1905, throwing three complete-game shutouts at the Philadelphia Athletics. Mathewson's numbers in New York's 4–1 Series victory: 3–0, 0.00 ERA, 27 innings, 14 hits, one walk, 18 strikeouts.

5. D) Rabbit Maranville   (*5 points*)

Maranville had 672 at bats for Pittsburgh in 1922 and didn't hit a homer. In more than 10,000 career at bats, this Hall of Fame shortstop hit just 28 home runs.

6. Mickey Mantle   (*4 points*)

Mickey Mantle finished second in the MVP balloting in both 1960 and 1961. "The Mick" was second to none as the MVP in 1962. He also won the award in 1956 and '57.

7. John Olerud, Paul Molitor, and Roberto Alomar
(*6 points*)

Toronto Blue Jays Olerud, Molitor, and Alomar were the top three hitters in the American League in 1993. In addition to winning a world championship, this trio also produced the league leader in hits (Molitor), doubles (Olerud), and on-base percentage (Olerud).

8. B) Eddie Murray   (*4 points*)

Murray drove in 996 runs during the decade, but was only able to win one RBI title—with 78 in the strike-shortened season of 1981.

9. Smokey Joe Wood   (*6 points*)

In addition to compiling a career 117–57 record and a 2.03 ERA, Wood became a fulltime outfielder after suffering a broken thumb, and batted .366 for Cleveland in 1921.

10. A) Monte Irvin   (*4 points*)

Irvin, a star in the Negro Leagues, had several fine seasons with the New York Giants in the early 1950s. The fans voted him onto the National League All-Star squad in 1952, despite the fact that he had broken his leg in spring training and wound up missing most of the season.

11. D) John Wehner   (*5 points*)

Pittsburgh native John Wehner, who came to Three Rivers for baseball games as a boy, hit a two-run homer in the fifth inning off Jon Lieber (an ex-Buc) of the Cubs before 55,351 fans, a Three Rivers record for baseball. It was Wehner's only home run of the season and just the fourth of his career. The Pirates lost to the Cubs, 10–9.

12. Elroy Face (*6 points*)

So close, but it wasn't meant to be. Face only threw one inning over two games with Detroit after the trade, and his 1969 stint with Montreal was his last big league season.

13. Rogers Hornsby, George Sisler, and Ty Cobb (*5 points*)

Cobb turned in his final .400-plus season, batting .401, but fell far short of Sisler's AL-leading .420 mark. Hornsby ran away with the NL batting title by hitting .401, beating out Chicago's Ray Grimes by 47 points.

14. 1920 Chicago White Sox and 1971 Baltimore Orioles (*6 points*)

The Chisox had Red Faber (23), Lefty Williams (22), Eddie Cicotte (21), and Dickie Kerr (21). Following the season, both Williams and Cicotte were banned from baseball for their involvement in throwing the 1919 World Series. The Baltimore pitchers were Dave McNally with 21 wins and Jim Palmer, Mike Cuellar, and Pat Dobson with 20 each.

15. C) Lou Gehrig (*5 points*)

The Iron Horse achieved the feat in 1932. He helped the Yankees to a world championship that year, ranking in the American League's top five in runs, hits, homers, RBIs, walks, batting average, on-base percentage, and slugging average.

16. B) Harold Baines (*4 points*)

Harold Baines logged more than 1,000 games as a DH and more than 1,000 games in the outfield. Paul Molitor played 1,174 games as a DH, and his highest total at any other position was 791 at third base. Hal McRae became a full-time DH in 1976 and logged 1,427 of his 2,084 games as the designated hitter. Fittingly, McRae later became a hitting coach.

17. B) Jim Bottomley and Paul Waner (*5 points*)

On May 7, 1925, Bottomley lined to Pittsburgh's Glenn Wright, who made the unassisted triple killing. The next time the rare feat took place—May 30, 1927—the batter was Waner and the Cubs' Jimmy Cooney turned it.

18. Four (*6 points*)

Lou Gehrig finished fifth in the MVP voting in 1934, Chuck Klein finished second in 1933, and Ted Williams finished second in 1942 and 1947. Rogers Hornsby (1925), Jimmie Foxx (1933), Joe Medwick (1937), Mickey Mantle (1956), Frank Robinson (1966), and Carl Yastrzemski (1967) won MVPs following their Triple Crown seasons.

19. B) Darren Daulton (*4 points*)

Darren Daulton of the last-place Phillies led the NL with 109 RBIs in 1992. The Dodgers also finished in last place, but Mike Piazza only played in 21 games as a late-season call-up. The following year he drove in 112 in his first full season.

20. Graig Nettles (*5 points*)

Nettles hit 319 home runs as an American League third baseman. He had his best years with the Yankees, making five All-Star appearances, winning a home run title, and reaching the postseason five times between 1973–83.

Top 9th

1. Dick Bosman (*7 points*)

Bosman, an AL pitcher in the 1960s and '70s, raced and designed dragsters as a kid, and once finished second in the national championships.

2. B) Bob Gibson (*5 points*)

Gibson won seven straight World Series starts in 1964, 1967, and 1968. His numbers over the three World Series: 7–2, eight complete games, 81 innings, 92 strikeouts, 1.89 ERA, two world championships.

3. Heinie Manush and Goose Goslin (*6 points*)

Manush, with the St. Louis Browns, was sent to the Washington Senators for Goslin, who slugged 30 homers for his new team and finished the campaign with a career-high 37.

4. B) 1894 Baltimore Orioles (*5 points*)

The 1894 Orioles had Hall of Famers Dan Brouthers at first, Hughie Jennings at short, and John McGraw at third. The second baseman was Heinie Reitz. The other three teams each sported two eventual Cooperstown inductees in their infields.

5. A) Lou Gehrig (*4 points*)

The Iron Horse did it 13 consecutive seasons, from 1926–38. Foxx is the runner-up with nine straight years, 1932–40.

6. 22–3 (*5 points*)

The Yankees lost two games to Cleveland in the '98 ALCS and one to Boston in the '99 ALCS. The three pitchers who beat them? Dave Burba, Bartolo Colon, and Pedro Martinez.

7. Tom Seaver and Nolan Ryan   (*6 points*)

Tom Seaver was named on 98.83 percent of the ballots in 1992, while Nolan Ryan was named on 98.79 percent of the ballots in 1999.

8. B) Cincinnati   (*4 points*)

The Reds and Orioles played the first World Series game on artificial turf in Cincinnati at what was then called Riverfront Stadium. The Reds lost the game, 4–3, and lost the Series in five. Busch Stadium in St. Louis, Veterans Stadium in Philadelphia, and Three Rivers Stadium in Pittsburgh were all hosting football instead of baseball in October 1970.

9. Dick Groat (*6 points*)

The 1960 National League MVP was a first-team All-American for Duke in both his junior and senior years. Groat also played one season of pro basketball with the Fort Wayne Pistons in 1952–53.

10. C) Grover Alexander   (*4 points*)

"Old Pete" Alexander posted winning records in 19 of his 20 seasons. Young, Spahn, and Ryan each did it 17 times, which ties them for second place.

11. B) Dick Drago   (*5 points*)

Dick Drago of the California Angels allowed Hank Aaron's last home run. The Brewers slugger connected on July 20, 1976. In 1974 Jack Billingham allowed Aaron's home run that tied him with Babe Ruth for the all-time record, and Al Downing surrendered the one that broke it. Jerry Augustine was a teammate of Aaron's in his final season with the Brewers.

12. Honus Wagner   (*4 points*)

Wagner won eight batting titles with the Pirates, including a stretch of seven titles in nine years. Tony Gwynn matched Wagner's NL record when he won his eighth title in 1997.

13. Stan Musial, Willie Mays, and Hank Aaron   (*5 points*)

Aaron played in his last All-Star Game in 1975 at age 41; Mays was an All-Star in 1973 at age 42; and Musial made his final All-Star appearance in 1963 at age 42.

14. Jim Bunning   (*5 points*)

Bunning's native Kentuckians elected him to the U.S. Senate in 1998. He was the first modern pitcher to win at least 100 games in both major leagues.

15. A) Jimmy Bannon (*5 points*)

Playing for Boston in the National League, the right fielder known as "Foxy Grandpa" hit grand slams on August 6 and 7, 1894. He was the only player to do it in the 19th century.

16. A) Bill Russell (*5 points*)

Dodgers shortstop Bill Russell singled home Ron Cey with the winning run in the 10th inning of Game 4. Cey had reached base when Philadelphia's Gold Glove center fielder Garry Maddox dropped a fly ball.

17. Frank Robinson (*4 points*)

Frank Robinson was a unanimous NL Rookie of the Year selection in 1956, when he hit 38 homers and scored 122 runs for Cincinnati. He won the Triple Crown his first year in Baltimore, 1966, hitting 49 homers and leading the league in runs, on-base percentage, and slugging average. Robinson was inducted into the Hall of Fame in 1982, along with Hank Aaron.

18. Bucky Walters (*6 points*)

Bucky Walters came up as a third baseman with the Boston Braves in 1931. After acquiring him in midseason in 1934, the Phillies tried out Walters on the mound. He only saw spot duty in the field after that, and went on to have three 20-win seasons in Cincinnati.

19. Willie Mays (*5 points*)

Mays won a World Series with the Giants in 1954, when he won the NL MVP at age 23, and didn't make it back to the Series until 1973, when he finished his career with the Mets at age 42.

20. D) Jimmie Foxx   (*4 points*)

Jimmie Foxx smacked 58 home runs in 1932, but "lost" two homers because two games were called before the fifth inning. "Double X" hit 534 career home runs, won the Triple Crown in 1933, and won the MVP Award three times, including 1932.

Bottom 9th

1. B) Rollie Fingers   (*3 points*)

Rollie Fingers not only won the 1981 AL MVP, he also won the Cy Young Award that year. For good measure, Fingers also received the AL Fireman of the Year Award in 1981, as the Brewers reached the postseason for the first time in team history.

2. M   (*4 points*)

Seven players whose last names begin with "M" have hit more than 400 home runs: Willie Mays, 660; Mark McGwire, 554; Mickey Mantle, 536; Willie McCovey, 521; Eddie Mathews, 512; Eddie Murray, 504; Stan Musial, 475.

3. C) Ken Williams   (*5 points*)

On April 22, 1922, Ken Williams of the St. Louis Browns was the first player in AL history to homer three times in one game. George Sisler was on base for all three homers. Williams also became the first 30-30 man in 1922, with 39 home runs and 37 stolen bases.

4. Dave Hansen (*5 points*)

On September 12, 2000, Dave Hansen broke a 68-year-old record by hitting his seventh pinch-hit homer of the season. Johnny Frederick hit six homers as a pinch hitter with the Brooklyn Dodgers in 1932.

5. Bill Dickey (*6 points*)

The Yankees catcher—who, like the five previous batters, was a future Hall of Famer—touched Hubbell for a single.

6. C) Gene Garber (*5 points*)

Gene Garber's sidearm delivery got Rose for the final out on July 31, 1978. Rose was annoyed at Garber's celebration after he struck him out to end the game. Rose noted that a celebration like Garber's looked like he'd "won the World Series."

7. 10 (*5 points*)

Ten if you count Yankees manager Miller Huggins. The players were Babe Ruth, Lou Gehrig, Tony Lazzeri, Earle Combs, Waite Hoyt, and Herb Pennock for the Yanks, and Paul Waner, Lloyd Waner, and Pie Traynor for the Pirates. Additionally, the Bucs had two other eventual Hall of Famers on their roster that year, Joe Cronin and Kiki Cuyler, but neither was with the team for the Series.

8. John Miller (*7 points*)

Miller debuted with a dinger for the Yankees on September 11, 1966. Three years later, in a Dodgers uniform, he hit a solo shot off Jim Merritt. It was his last at bat, and the two homers were the only ones he ever hit.

9. Rick Wise   (*7 points*)

Pitching for the Phillies on June 23, 1971, Wise no-hit Cincinnati while helping his cause with not one, but two home runs.

10. Philadelphia Phillies   (*5 points*)

The team's batting order featured Chuck Klein (.386, 40 HR, 170 RBIs) and Lefty O'Doul (.383, with a .453 OBP). The Phillies' downfall was their pitching staff, which finished the 1930 season with a 6.71 ERA.

11. Joe DiMaggio   (*5 points*)

DiMaggio accomplished the feat seven times. The Yankee Clipper's best season in this regard was 1941, the year of his 56-game hitting streak, when he smacked 30 homers and fanned only 13 times.

12. Grover Alexander   (*4 points*)

Alexander won Triple Crowns from 1915–17. Pitching for the Philadelphia Phillies, he strung together three straight seasons with 30 or more wins, making him the last pitcher of the century to accomplish that feat. His ERA was under 2.00 in all three seasons.

13. Rogers Hornsby   (*5 points*)

Hornsby hit .424 with the St. Louis Cardinals in 1924, .387 with the Boston Braves in 1928, and .380 with the Chicago Cubs in 1929.

14. Babe Ruth (*4 points*)

In 1920 the Bambino batted .376 with 54 home runs and 137 RBIs. All told, he accomplished the feat a record 12 times.

15. Tom Zachary (*6 points*)

Pitching for the Yankees in 1929, Zachary went 12–0. Two seasons before, while pitching for the Washington Senators, he gave up Babe Ruth's 60th home run.

16. Rogers Hornsby (*5 points*)

The Rajah hit .401 in 1922, and his 42 home runs remained a major league record for second basemen until Davey Johnson hit 43 in 1973.

17. C) Lave Cross (*5 points*)

In 1902 the star third baseman of the Philadelphia A's had 108 RBIs and no home runs. He'd had a similar showing in 1895, when he drove in 101 with only a pair of homers.

18. Ozzie Smith (*5 points*)

Everyone was leaving the yard in 1987 except Ozzie Smith. The Wizard drove in 75 runs without hitting a homer, leading the Cardinals to a pennant.

19. D) Hi Myers (*5 points*)

The Brooklyn Dodgers outfielder eked out his title with 73 RBIs in 1919, barely edging Rogers Hornsby and Edd Roush, who each had 71.

20. Chuck Klein (*4 points*)

In 1933 Klein won the Triple Crown and led the NL in doubles, on-base percentage, and slugging average. For all his success, the Phillies traded him to the Chicago Cubs on November 21 for Mark Koenig, Harvey Hendrick, rookie Ted Kleinhans, and $125,000.

	1	2	3	4	5	6	7	8	9	F
VISITORS										
HOME										

SCORESHEET

TOP 1st

1.____   6.____   11.____   16.____

2.____   7.____   12.____   17.____

3.____   8.____   13.____   18.____   **INNING TOTAL____**

4.____   9.____   14.____   19.____

5.____   10.____   15.____   20.____

BOTTOM 1st

1.____   6.____   11.____   16.____

2.____   7.____   12.____   17.____

3.____   8.____   13.____   18.____   **INNING TOTAL____**

4.____   9.____   14.____   19.____

5.____   10.____   15.____   20.____

TOP 2nd

1.____   6.____   11.____   16.____

2.____   7.____   12.____   17.____

3.____   8.____   13.____   18.____   **INNING TOTAL____**

4.____   9.____   14.____   19.____

5.____   10.____   15.____   20.____

BOTTOM 2nd

1.___	6.___	11.___	16.___	
2.___	7.___	12.___	17.___	
3.___	8.___	13.___	18.___	**INNING TOTAL**___
4.___	9.___	14.___	19.___	
5.___	10.___	15.___	20.___	

TOP 3rd

1.___	6.___	11.___	16.___	
2.___	7.___	12.___	17.___	
3.___	8.___	13.___	18.___	**INNING TOTAL**___
4.___	9.___	14.___	19.___	
5.___	10.___	15.___	20.___	

BOTTOM 3rd

1.___	6.___	11.___	16.___	
2.___	7.___	12.___	17.___	
3.___	8.___	13.___	18.___	**INNING TOTAL**___
4.___	9.___	14.___	19.___	
5.___	10.___	15.___	20.___	

TOP 4th

1.___	6.___	11.___	16.___	
2.___	7.___	12.___	17.___	
3.___	8.___	13.___	18.___	**INNING TOTAL**___
4.___	9.___	14.___	19.___	
5.___	10.___	15.___	20.___	

BOTTOM 4th

1.___	6.___	11.___	16.___	
2.___	7.___	12.___	17.___	
3.___	8.___	13.___	18.___	**INNING TOTAL___**
4.___	9.___	14.___	19.___	
5.___	10.___	15.___	20.___	

TOP 5th

1.___	6.___	11.___	16.___	
2.___	7.___	12.___	17.___	
3.___	8.___	13.___	18.___	**INNING TOTAL___**
4.___	9.___	14.___	19.___	
5.___	10.___	15.___	20.___	

BOTTOM 5th

1.___	6.___	11.___	16.___	
2.___	7.___	12.___	17.___	
3.___	8.___	13.___	18.___	**INNING TOTAL___**
4.___	9.___	14.___	19.___	
5.___	10.___	15.___	20.___	

TOP 6th

1.___	6.___	11.___	16.___	
2.___	7.___	12.___	17.___	
3.___	8.___	13.___	18.___	**INNING TOTAL___**
4.___	9.___	14.___	19.___	
5.___	10.___	15.___	20.___	

BOTTOM 6th

1.___	6.___	11.___	16.___	
2.___	7.___	12.___	17.___	
3.___	8.___	13.___	18.___	INNING TOTAL_____
4.___	9.___	14.___	19.___	
5.___	10.___	15.___	20.___	

TOP 7th

11.___	6.___	11.___	16.___	
2.___	7.___	12.___	17.___	
3.___	8.___	13.___	18.___	INNING TOTAL_____
4.___	9.___	14.___	19.___	
5.___	10.___	15.___	20.___	

BOTTOM 7th

11.___	6.___	11.___	16.___	
2.___	7.___	12.___	17.___	
3.___	8.___	13.___	18.___	INNING TOTAL_____
4.___	9.___	14.___	19.___	
5.___	10.___	15.___	20.___	

TOP 8th

1.___	6.___	11.___	16.___	
2.___	7.___	12.___	17.___	
3.___	8.___	13.___	18.___	INNING TOTAL_____
4.___	9.___	14.___	19.___	
5.___	10.___	15.___	20.___	

BOTTOM 8th

1.____	6.____	11.____	16.____	
2.____	7.____	12.____	17.____	
3.____	8.____	13.____	18.____	**INNING TOTAL**_____
4.____	9.____	14.____	19.____	
5.____	10.____	15.____	20.____	

TOP 9th

1.____	6.____	11.____	16.____	
2.____	7.____	12.____	17.____	
3.____	8.____	13.____	18.____	**INNING TOTAL**_____
4.____	9.____	14.____	19.____	
5.____	10.____	15.____	20.____	

BOTTOM 9th

1.____	6.____	11.____	16.____	
2.____	7.____	12.____	17.____	
3.____	8.____	13.____	18.____	**INNING TOTAL**_____
4.____	9.____	14.____	19.____	
5.____	10.____	15.____	20.____	